QUEEN OF ALL THE DUSTBALLS
and other epics of everyday life

BILL RICHARDSON

Illustrations by
Bill Horne

POLESTAR
BOOK PUBLISHERS

Poems and Introduction © 1992 by Bill Richardson
Illustrations © 1992 by Bill Horne

Published by
Polestar Press Ltd
P.O. Box 69382, Station K
Vancouver, B.C.
V5K 4W6

Distributed in Canada by
Raincoast Books
112 East Third Avenue
Vancouver, B.C.
V5T 1C8

Published through the financial assistance of the Canada
Council and British Columbia Cultural Services Branch

Cover design by Jim Brennan
Author photo by Daniel Collins
Production by Michelle Benjamin
Printed in Canada

Canadian Cataloguing in Publication Data
Richardson, Bill, 1955-
Queen of all the dustballs and other epics of everyday life

Poems.
ISBN 0-919591-98-1

1. Humorous poetry, Canadian (English). I. Title

PS8585.I186Q84 1992   C811'.54   C92-090559-4
PR9199.3.R43Q84   1992

CONTENTS

But if poetry is left to poets, it means that something else, picking apples, say, is left to the apple pickers, and not only don't we get good poems about harvesting apples, we get a society that believes that apple pickers can't write poetry — which is what we have.

— *Sue Halpern, Migrations to Solitude*

Introduction
by Romana Clay, R.N.

In November, 19__, I was working a night shift in the Emergency Ward of St._____ Hospital—a major depot for the ushering in, the ushering out, and the between-times maintenance of the citizens of V_____. It had been a night like any other: a 12-hour stretch, punctuated by visits from those afflicted with the various attacks, arrests, stoppages, seizures, bruises, welts, and abrasions to which we are all heir by dint of the fact that we are made of flesh. Babies with high fevers. Teenagers deafened by wax build-up. Next day lunch-makers with nasty cuts from the serrated edges of tin foil boxes. Industrial equipment operators who had not heeded the drowsiness warnings on their sinus medication, and who now prayed fervently for reattachment. Light bulbs and pop bottles inhabiting places they were never intended to live.

This is the job I have done for more than ten years. "How can you bear it?" my friends and family ask. "Doesn't the mayhem wear you down? Aren't you burned out? Don't you despair to see the endless parade of tragedy and folly?"

The simple answer is no. This is my country, my grammar, my currency. These are my people. I am not a tourist here. And other than the exploitation of the weak by the mighty, there is little that can shock or appall me, or make me wish I had landed on the planet as a vegetable or mineral. To be sure, there are times when I feel slightly world-weary, and I think I have seen it all: that I have encountered every possible manifestation of human aberrance, that there are no challenges or surprises remaining. But something always comes along to jar me out of my complacency. On the November night of which I speak, a man walked, alone and unassisted, into my Emergency Ward. He seemed average in every respect, save for one glaring oddity. Protruding from the middle of his forehead was what I took at first glance to be an antler. A second glance, and then a third, revealed the startling appendage to be, in fact, a crevice tool: a simple vacuum cleaner attachment rendered extraordinary only because it was affixed, by some miracle of suction that flew in the face of the laws of physics, to the "between the eyes" portion of the patient's head. He seemed a little out of sorts, as well you can imagine. However, he was experiencing no real physical discomfort, and all his vital signs were strong and steady. While we waited for a doctor to come and devise a way of wresting the tool from its unfortunate roost, I took down a brief history. It was tempting to ask the most obvious question straight off the bat; but I am, above all else, a professional. I know that first things must come first. Let me reconstruct, to the best of my ability, the beginnings of what has subsequently proved to be a very long conversation.

"Your name?"

"You don't recognize me?"

"I'm afraid not."

"Oh. I'm Bill Richardson."

(This information he imparted with the reverent tones of a jeweller assuring his client that the diamond was housed in a platinum setting.)

"And I would take it that you are a vacuum cleaner salesman?"

"Oh ho ho ho ho! What a kidder you are, Nurse!"

"I beg your pardon?"

"A vacuum cleaner salesman! Go on!"

"I'm sorry Mr. Richardson. I should never have presumed. What **is** your occupation, then?"

"You mean—you've never heard of me?"

"I'm afraid not."

"Never, not once?"

"No," I replied with a shake of my head.

"Damn! Isn't that just bloody typical? Isn't that just about what you'd expect? A prophet in his own country! Unrecognized! Dishonoured! For your information, Nurse, I am the self-appointed Poet Laureate of Canada. It's a dirty job, but somebody's got to do it."

As I have suggested, it takes a great deal to make me blanch.

However, one of the reasons I became a nurse is that—until the evening of this fateful encounter—I fainted at the sight of literature. For as long as I can remember, I reacted to meter and rhyme in much the same way some allergy sufferers respond to bee stings. For the whole of my life, to that point in any case, the overhearing of the slightest poetic utterance— "Break, break, break on thy cold grey stones oh sea!" or "Whose woods these are I think I know"—was sufficient to precipitate in me a cold sweat and a gelling of the knees, enough to pitch me into the deepest slough of despond. I never sought out the wellspring of this pathology. I only know it was real.

You can appreciate then, that the idea of sharing a small, enclosed space, such as an emergency ward examining cubicle, with a self-proclaimed and practising poet was almost more than I could stomach. I had to summon up every ounce of professional vigour to prevent myself from running, gagging, from the room. I could feel the blood draining from my cheeks, and I've no doubt that a terrible pallor washed over my face. Anyone less self-absorbed than a poet with a crevice tool stuck to his forehead would have noted the change in my complexion, and summoned aid, or at the very least suggested that I put my head between my knees. But the patient was so thoroughly engrossed in his own dilemma that I might simply have been a rose, fading on the wallpaper. I let my concentration slide from his mutterings and focused instead on quieting the insurgent rebellion that was rumbling through my gastrointestinal tract.

How much time elapsed? Not more than a minute or two, surely. Deep breathing and a supreme effort of will pulled me back from the edge of the abyss. I directed my attentions once again to the patient and his narrative. By now, the poet God had so cruelly thrust into my keeping was sliding along some remote and slippery tangent. His breath was shallow and rapid and, I might add, rather redolent of whisky. His eyes had a wild and feral look, such as might come over the orbs of a coyote who had been caught in a leghold trap, and who knows with some instinctive certainty that the angel of death hovers in the near vicinity. A stream of nonsense words spilled from his lips. He made me think of the miller's daughter who becomes Queen by way of elfish interference, and then must guess the name of Rumplestiltskin, or else surrender her son.

"Dustball, rusthall, justball, cussdoll. . ."

I am ashamed of what happened next. Something in me snapped. Every remembrance of Hippocrates, every souvenir of the ethics course at which I excelled at nursing school, was trampled by a stampede of conflicting emotions: horror, fascination, repulsion, compassion. I could see no other course than to take radical action.

I am persuaded that had I had a syringe near to hand, and the necessary compounds to mix a lethal injection, I would have done so, and administered it first to him and then to me. As it was, I simply lifted a hand and slapped him, hard, first on the left cheek, then on the right. I grabbed him by the shoulders, and shook him as though he were a broken bubblegum dispenser, and foamed these words:

"How did you get a goddamn crevice tool stuck to your forehead?"

This was drastic and reprehensible but, as it turned out, effective. The poet's bumper car thoughts locked on a single track. For a moment, lucidity reigned.

"Isn't it an amazing thing, the crevice tool?" he said, suddenly calm and rational. He went on to deliver himself of the following lecture in exactly the tone of voice an elementary school science teacher might use to extol the wonders of pond water.

"There are several things that astonish me about the crevice tool. One is that it exists at all. That someone perceived the need for such a device, designed and patented it, then arranged for its manufacture and distribution, engenders in me nothing less than a frisson of delight. Even more awe-inspiring is the fact that that anonymous genius chose to name his or her invention the "crevice tool" and, insofar as history records, no one has ever thought to so much as bat an eye. But why, Nurse? Why? Does no one else find "crevice tool" a rather unseemly appellation? Think of it, Nurse! Day after day, men and women the nation over go out to work, leaving spouses, children, pets, alone in the house with something called a "crevice tool." Do they never contemplate the vast potential for harm that exists in such a situation? Am I the only person in all of Christendom who is driven to near distraction by this evidence of the trust and regard we have for one another?"

His eyes were starting to roll back in their sockets. His head lolled on the stem of his neck, like a parched daisy. I slapped him again, two stinging blows, noting as I did so how his nostril hairs quivered, giving him a look of something that approached vulnerability.

"But how? How did it get attached to your forehead?"

Again, normalcy, or its close facsimile, surfaced. He showed no sign of objecting to, or even noticing, the way he had just been nursehandled. I watched the bruises deepen on his face as he offered the following, bizarre explanation.

"I am writing an epic ode in which the crevice tool plays a pivotal role. It is called the "Queen of All the Dustballs," and it is, I venture to say, my *chef d'oeuvre*. However, I have been defeated in my efforts to find the right rhyme for dustball. I thought that if I were to meditate upon the problem, with a crevice tool held to my third eye, to the psychic receptor, to what some might call the head chakra, it might prove a conduit for inspiration from beyond."

"But against my every expectation, when I tried to lower it, it couldn't be budged. It is fixed fast, like Excalibur in the stone. What am I to do? Go through life looking like a unicorn in search of a virgin? Why has this happened? Why has some malevolent force chosen this moment to play a cruel joke? I've always known that you run certain risks when you're a toyboy for the muse! What will become of me now? A crevice tool stuck to my head, no rhyme for dustball, and a deadline to boot."

He disintegrated into the tears which I took to be a sure prelude to an even more profound breakdown.

Gentle Reader. When I tell you what happened next, you will surely be tempted to hurl this little book to the floor, and trample it into the broadloom. You will certainly think that I have taken the already tenuous taffy of credibility, and stretched it to the breaking point. I must ask you though, to suspend your disbelief. I am doing nothing but reporting the bald facts. You would do well to gird yourselves, psychically speaking, with the words of Emily Dickinson, a poet who never—as near as we know—had an untoward encounter with a crevice tool. Recall how she wrote that "after great pain, a formal feeling comes / The nerves sit ceremonious, like tombs."

The Belle of Amherst told it like it is. Great pain, a formal feeling: at that very moment, in the pounding midst of the emotional storm that was raging all around me, I was visited by a sense of peace, calm and purpose such as I have never known. It was as if I could look both ways down the long and echoing corridor of time and see very clearly every bit of graffiti scrawled on those walls: what had been, what is, what will be.

A voice spoke in my ear. "Be not afraid," it said. "You are blessed among nurses." And hearing the voice pronounce the word "nurses" engendered the kind of epiphany that comes along perhaps once in a lifetime. I understood, all at once, that "nurses", phonetically speaking, is a mere consonant removed from "verses"; that healing is not the sole province of medicine; that literature is a balm, and that poetry especially is a sulpha drug for the spirit; and that this raving nutter and his rogue crevice tool had been sent to me for a purpose.

Then and there, the fear of poetry that had dogged me all my days, was lifted from me. Gone were the blinding scales. Lanced was the poxy boil. I felt full and powerful. I turned to the Poet, looked him squarely in the eye, and said in a voice that was not my own, and in words that were not of my choosing—"The rhyme you need is 'must call.'" Then I laid hands on the crevice tool, and removed it from his forehead as easily as I might have plucked a plum. Inspired by who knows what power, I placed the thing to my lips and blew a loud and clarion note. In the twinkling of an eye, all was changed. My life and his were inextricably entwined. Nothing would ever be the same again.

Addendum
by Bill Richardson, B.A.

The objective facts reported by Nurse Clay are accurate. Only she can swear to the veracity of her spiritual odyssey; I have no reason to cast doubt or aspersions on her account.

The cleaving of the crevice tool, which she has so poignantly described, occurred as I was endeavouring to finish a poem for broadcast on CBC Radio's *Gabereau* programme, hosted by the lovely and ever so eponymous Vicki Gabereau. There are not many places where a self-appointed Poet Laureate can make a living. *Gabereau* is one of them. For several years prior to this peculiar incident of unsolicited adhesion, I had penned odes for listeners who would write to me with events in their lives they wanted commemorated in doggerel verse: birthdays, weddings, anniversaries, family reunions. You know the kind of thing I mean.

A woman in Toronto had requested a cautionary tale for her neat freak brother, Bob. I was moved to write an ode called "Queen of All the Dustballs." This was the epic on which I was embarked when the incident described by Romana Clay occurred. When you read the poem, you will see that, in fact, "must call" was exactly what was needed to rhyme with "dustball."

Nurse Clay's intervention—more mystical than medical—has indeed thrown us together. Perhaps the best way to describe our present relationship is "mutual shamanism." I have, in some small way, nudged her along the lovely and winding path of poetry. She has become a champion of my *oeuvre*, and a kind of muse as well. Subsequent to our initial encounter, there have been times without number when she has pried from the universe the exact rhyme or turn of phrase I needed to buff up a poem, and turn it into a bright and shining thing.

Each of the poems in this volume was inspired by a letter from a listener. Alas, these missives—which were carefully filed—were lost in a whirlwind. Happily, Nurse Clay, using a combination of dream analysis, hypnotherapy, shiatsu, and the occasional administering of single malt whiskeys, has been able to extract from between the folds of what passes for my brain the approximate details of the stories that spawned the poems. Romana has written the brief notes explaining the occasion for each poem, but I am solely responsible for any inaccuracies therein contained.

Thanks then to those listeners who wrote asking for poems, and to request copies of the verses they heard on the radio; to Michelle Benjamin and Julian Ross; to my colleagues at CBC Radio; to Romana Clay, R.N.; and most particularly to Vicki Gabereau, to whom this little book is dedicated, with real love and affection.

QUEEN OF ALL THE DUSTBALLS

The circumstances surrounding the composition of this poem, arguably Mr. Richardson's most complex to date, have been alluded to in the Introduction. A Toronto woman asked for a cautionary tale, a little bagatelle to warn her neat freak brother against the dangers of excessive pernicketiness. How could she have guessed that her innocuous request would generate this stunning saga, bristling with Arthurian allusions? But then—who among us can understand the ways of the Muse?

Once—not very long ago and not so far away—
Lived a man called Bob who, at the dawning of each day,
Vowed to rid the world of grime and keep it all pristine.
He'd dab his dainty wrists and lobes with Vim and Mr. Clean,
Then don his starched and ironed jeans and freshly-laundered shirt,
And stride out in the germy world to vanquish filth and dirt.
No spill nor stain nor stinking drain would valiant Bob deter:
He'd fight them with his trusty sponge, and mop, Excalibur.
He had a potent vacuum he would use for heavy jobs,
And any guy would die to have a crevice tool like Bob's.
So long, so wide, so true, so tried, imbued with lasting power,
The kind of tool to make you drool and run a chilling shower.
(But that's enough of all this stuff. I'll get myself in trouble:
You'll think I'm crude if I intrude with rude *entendre doubles*.)
Let's hearken back to Bob and to the story that's at hand:
His mission was to purge the scourge of dirt throughout the land.
He'd travel through the countryside and challenge every mess,
He had a thousand solvents to alleviate distress.
If gallant lords and damsels couldn't cope with rampant dustballs,
They never had the slightest doubt that it was Bob they must call.

A breathless runner one day came, his ruby lips were trembling.
"How now brown cow?" asked noble Bob, no need of fear dissembling.
"Oh Master Bob," the runner sobbed, his eyes all wild and feral,
"We have construed, oh fearsome news, our nation is in peril!
I do not sing of petty things, of cash or constitutions,
But rather of a dustball who's demanding restitution.
No, not some pallid, squalid ball that lurks beneath the bed,
No tiny hallway tumbleweed," the frightened runner said.
"No, this is one mean Mama with a mean gleam in her eye.
She's Yukon cold and twice as big again as P.E.I.!
She's called you names like git and twit and nit and even slob!
She's Queen of All the Dustballs and she's out to get you, Bob!"
"Oh is that so? Ho ho! Ho ho!" cried Bob. "Well let her threaten!
That dusty yob has not met Bob, nor faced his fearsome weapons!
My faithful mop Excalibur will end her grisly rule:
The dreadful wretch won't soon forget my mighty crevice tool!"

So out Bob strode, along the road, cheered on by gladsome crowds.
He swaggered full of confidence, erect, correct, and proud.
As David slew Goliath and as Beowulf offed Grendel,
Bob was preened to meet the Queen and show she could be handled.
He smelled her ere he saw her and he gaped at what he saw:
A tangled mass of clinging dirt around a gaping maw.
She had a tumbling swagger and she had a taunting sneer:
She pulsed and loomed and then she boomed:

"HEY BOB! GET OVER HERE!
I SEE YOU'VE BROUGHT SOME TOYS ALONG IN ORDER TO DEFEAT ME!
IS THAT YOUR FAMOUS CREVICE TOOL?
OR ARE YOU PLEASED TO MEET ME?"
"Oh foul wretch," big Bob kvetched, "from what dank grave exhumed?
Now leave our land! No man will stand to hear his tool impugned!"

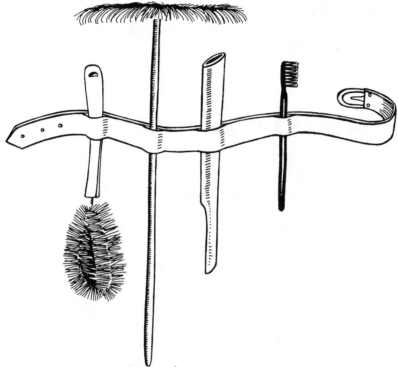

So fell they to. I know that you have never ever seen
So grim a sight as was the fight of Robert and the Queen.
He dashed her with Excalibur, she countered every charge.
Their vicious words were clearly heard from here to Lake Labarge.
He doused her with ammonia and she uttered piercing shrieks.
She filled his lungs with dust and dung till Bob, once strong, grew weak.
From brute to wimp, all wilted, limp, he spent his warrior lust:
She showed no ruth but proved the truth that no man's match for dust.

Bob will never more be seen. His mission has been squelched.
His only sordid epitaph was when the Dust Queen belched.
My tale is done. The moral is one that's very plain to see:
Dust is how you started out and dust is what you'll be.

LAUNDRY VENDREDI

A woman in Vancouver wrote to say that her friends thought her peculiar for spurning social engagements on Friday evenings in order to attend to her laundry. The careful reader will note here how well Mr. Richardson learned from the "dustball / must call" epiphany. His choice of "day flagged" and "Maytag," as well as "new genes" and "blue jeans" demonstrates that it was a lesson he took, perhaps too closely, to heart.

On Friday nights, when most folks tend to caper and to scamper,
I choose to in my small apartment bide.
At 8 o'clock I take my bulging, fetid wicker hamper,
And double date with Fleecy and with Tide.
I segregate my garments and my twisted sheets and towels,
Darks together, quite distinct from white,
Then hump them twenty storeys down, and there within the bowels
Of my building spend my Friday night.
I know this may sound sad to you, but you would be mistaken
To judge my social prospects wan and lean.
I do not feel bereft, alone, forgotten or forsaken
But revel in the chance to render clean
The clothing of the bygone week: the shirts and socks and undies.
I love to purge them of their blots and stains,
And stride into the weekend feeling well prepared for Monday,
When work will rear its ugly head again.
And oh my wilted spirits which throughout the livelong day flagged
Start to sing the moment that I pause
To readjust the settings on the slightly battered Maytags,
And open up their happy, gaping maws.
I pile my cheesy items in, and add in heaping measure
The soap that longs to purge them of their sins.
I ply the slots with quarters, feel again the surging pleasure
That comes on me as soon as Wash begins.
Oh, the warm and happy spill, the burble of the geyser
The swish and slosh, the atavistic gush
Makes me feel as happy as a cash-encumbered miser,
Engendering a near-erotic rush.

The vision of the steaming stew of tablecloths and blue jeans
Brings to mind the great primordial jam,
Where somehow nascent DNA assembled into new genes
And, as I understand it, life began.
The cycles turn to rinse and spin. The washer's mad fandango
Bumps and grinds and shudders to a halt.
Now the dryers want to trot their hot and frenzied tango,
And play their part in laundry night gestalt.
They have their price: a loonie, please. I pay the eager floozies,
And straight away they start to hum and prance.
They're none of them attractive, but a beggar can't be choosy
Or rue the day a dime would buy a dance.
It takes them forty minutes to perform the whole routine.
My eyes, I must confess, soon lose their glint.
While waiting I might have a smoke or read a magazine,
Or meditate upon the coming lint.
The lint's my favourite part of all: the laundry's crowning glory.
I thrill to see the trap and all it bears.
I love to peel the dross away, to fabricate a story
Explaining why each hint of lint is there.
Was this an errant Kleenex that was hidden in the pocket?
A ticket stub, or transfer? Who can tell?
I know that this is weirdness and you'll feel compelled to mock it
But lint's my passion. You can go to hell.
I fold my toasty laundry and ascend to my apartment,
Restore my drawers to drawers, and hang my shirts,
Pat the cat and go to bed, the model of comportment,
My vestments all divested of all dirt.
And steeped in this accomplishment I lie, supine, contented,
Waiting there for sleep, whose tread is stealthy.
It's nine o'clock. My laundry's done. My sheets are crisp and scented—
All is clean. I hope my dreams are filthy.

THE BEST-LAID PLUMS

A straightforward poetic rendering of a prose narrative. This is one of two poems in this collection which deal with preserves: a demonstration of Mr. Richardson's fondness for condiments of all kinds.

Empowered by a vision of a chill dark winter night,
A thousand leagues removed from summer's heady, sweet delights,
And driven by the certainty of frosted, barren branch,
A bleeding cold no weakened sun could cauterize or stanch,
We looked for ways we might subvert the dying of the year
By capturing, before she fled , some summer souvenir,
Some something to remember her before she us forsook:
We could have pressed her flowers in some ancient weighty book,
Or taken many photographs before she'd run her span
Of tennis games and barbecues and you and me with tans.
Instead, our way of besting winter when he came to spar
Was culling fruits and vegetables and putting them in jars.
Oh what a lovely sight we conjured! Row on pristine row
Of peaches hung like little suns in syrup. By their glow
We'd see our jams and jellies safe from brutish, callous Time
We'd see our plum preserves and pickles happy in their brine,
We'd see our apple butter and our chutney's tender blush:
And summer's sweet, sweet long ago would flood back in a rush.
The fever was upon us then. We'd fanned the canning fire:
We nipped to that all-purpose store—I mean Canadian Tire,
And purchased jars and kettles for a hefty sum of loot,
Then started to amass the sundry vegetables and fruit.
We set aside a weekend for the project. We began
With much the same enthusiasm God evinced for man
And woman when he rented them his garden green and dappled:
A paradise they wrecked by their intemperance with an apple.
Had we but thought upon that myth we might well have construed
That tampering with fruits would also prove our Waterloo.

We plunged the fuzzy peaches in the frothy, boiling bath,
They must have thought inquisitors were venting pent-up wrath:
We peeled them and we pitted them and sliced and diced them too
And bunged them each in steaming vats of sugared, sticky goo.
And likewise we attacked the plums, and likewise mauled the pears,
We dilled the beans and cukes, dispatched the apples from their cares.
The kitchen was a battle zone, all thick with layers of gore:
Juice and skin and stickiness and bits of seed and core.
We laboured 12 hours Saturday. The Sabbath saw no rest,
But Sunday night our pantry shelves could stand beside the best.
For there, all neatly on display and glistening in their ranks
Ranged our jars of summer. We breathed deeply and gave thanks,
And toasted our achievements, soaked with sweat and sore with strain,
By opening a bottle of some Spanish cheap champagne.
We'd scarcely clinked our glasses when we heard a dreadful din:
We'd left the kitchen door ajar to let the kitty in,
Without anticipating that our wares would meet their end
When kitty brought a puppy home. Her panting canine friend
Had a long and ropy leash that from his collar dangled,
And when the leash with wonky shelves got knotted and entangled
Our jars of fruits and vegetables that bred in us euphoria
Met a sharded, sordid end. Ah well. *Sic transit gloria.*
We'd cleaned it up by 3 AM. By 4 we were in bed,
Visions, not of sugar plums, kept romping through our heads.
Summer's gone. Tonight I felt the first chill winter draft.
Our pantry's filled up with preserves. The labels all read Kraft.

THE RESOUNDING TINKLE

Mrs. Taggart, of Gloucester, Ontario, phoned Mr. Richardson one day (collect) at the CBC. Over the course of a very lengthy conversation, she observed that the phone always rings when one is in the midst of performing personal ablutions. Would Mr. Richardson compose a poem about this phenomenon? He did.

Scientists are prone to feuds, but every warring faction
Understands the principle of action and reaction.
It's push and pull. It's yin and yang. It's Mary and it's Rhoda.
Action and reaction are as twinned as scotch and soda.
When one takes place, the other can in no way be deterred:
Opposite, and equal, it is certain to occur.
For instance—if I lean my weight against a swinging door,
An aperture will open where there wasn't one before.
Action and reaction. It's a simple minded notion:
The pulling of the moon engenders tides within the ocean,
The shining of the sun produces melting of the snow:
"Alright, alright," I hear you cry, "We know! We know! We know!"
I know that this is obvious and that is why you're terse.
But there's another force at work throughout the universe
That uses this same principle. I'll brook no rude rebuttal
In telling you this self-same force is cunning, sly, and subtle.
I've seen it time and time again. Each time it makes me madder:
The phone will opt to ring when I decide to drain my bladder.
It makes me want to shout and scream, to ululate and howl
The way it tintinnabulates each time I move my bowels.
It's so perverse. It's so bizarre. Whatever can I do
To understand how phones are linked to number one and two?
Here's the way it seems to work. You drink a pot of tea
In blessed silence, undisturbed, then feel the urge to pee.
The phone hangs in the kitchen, white and silent as a nun.
It hasn't rung all evening. Not one phone call. No. Not one.
You say a little prayer for luck: this moment, Lord, is precious,
Don't let the phone intrude upon the pause they say refreshes.
You tiptoe to the porcelain, unbutton, pull and dangle:

And at that very moment it is jangle jangle jangle.
A panic rises in you then. You hold a smoking gun.
You can't turn off the faucet till it's had a chance to run.
You can't arrest the plumbing. It is stubborn and resistant.
The phone emits its seventh ring. The caller is persistent.
"Come on, come on," you mutter, feeling panicked and frenetic,
Both of which are feelings that are anti-diuretic.
The flow becomes a trickle as the river feeds the lake.
"I'll be there in a jiffy!" you exclaim, "I'll be two shakes!"
You give it three. The proverb says in truth, "Though you may dance
The evidence of where you've been is spotted on your pants."
The toilet's flushed, the family jewels are locked back in the vault.
You reach the phone the moment it decides to call a halt.
"Hello, hello!" you shout in vain against the braying tone.
Somewhere, someone shrugs and says, "I guess he isn't home."
I've seen it all too often now, had many demonstrations:
Action and reaction. Ringing phones. Elimination.
Can someone help me fix this, or invent a potent tonic
To sever my biology from noisy telephonics?
To go uninterrupted seems to me a worthwhile goal:
Is it too much to ask for this when I'm astride the bowl?
I know you think the simple way to find relief from tension
Is simply to install a handy, toiletside extension.
True enough. But what a chore to always be explaining
Why, when people call, they hear the sound of gentle raining.
I think perhaps a better way to free me of these fetters
Is disconnect the bloody phone, communicate through letters.
And if they spawn the same response—so what? It's no big issue,
I'll read them in the bathroom, then recycle them as tissue.

TOILET TRAINING LULLABY

A mother from the Okanagan Valley wrote to Mr. Richardson describing, in glorious detail, the difficulties she was having training her otherwise precocious two year old daughter to use the toilet. Her problems were exacerbated by the child's two grandmothers, who were becoming rather arch about the woman's seeming inability to ween her child from diapers. It was a charming letter, and Mr. Richardson was moved to compose an equally charming verse. The observant reader will notice a kind of scatalogical theme developing at this point in the collection. Fear not. It won't last long.

Darling dumpling, baby mine,
Deep in slumber's arms entwined,
Through the dreamtime woods you scamper
Swathed in nothing but a Pamper.

In those dreamy woods streams burble:
Now I hear your stomach gurgle.
Now I scent the waftings strange:
Time for yet another change.

Eight months past you learned to walk.
Two more months and you could talk.
Time is moving ever faster,
Only one skill left to master.

Darling you are nearly two.
By this time you know when you
Put on a diaper, and soil it
I must dump it in the toilet.

Let's declare a stern embargo
On those diapers and their cargo.
Hearing nature's clarion call,
Skip into the loo. That's all.

Time and time again I've said that.
Time and time I've read that
Children take their own sweet time.
Dumpling—are you near your prime?

Mr. Spock and Mr. Freud
Say I mustn't be annoyed.
They have warned my pleadings vain'll
Only brew fixations anal.

I should never like to think
One day that some future shrink
Might declare your ego smothered
By an overbearing mother.

I have read that all the functions
You perform with such great gumption
Are creative in their essence:
Not just oozing, foul excrescence.

Be assured then, I'm enthralled
By your murals on the wall.
Who else, at your tender age,
Makes such cunning use of beige?

Who would dare to stanch the surges
Of these first creative urges?
No one, save your nagging nanas.
Both are driving me bananas.

When they grill me yet again,
Let us sit down and explain
All that's psychological
In habits scatological.

Then, when next they gripe in turn:
"Will that baby ever learn?"
I shall rear up in defiance,
Show them you excel in science!

Though it's true you will not deign
To ascend the bubbling drain,
You demonstrate precocity
And looming curiosity.

Early on you figured out
How to make the whirling spout,
How to make the pleasing rush,
How to work the body flush!

You have managed to deposit
Half the items from my closet
In the white and glistening bowl.
You have taken quite a toll:

Flushing shoes as well as sandals,
Swooshing bell and book and candle.
You have bid farewell to coasters,
Risked your life to dunk the toaster,

Tried to flush away the dog.
Twice a week you plug the bog.
Plumbers know just where our place is,
And we're on a first name basis.

Baby, think me not a griper.
You look cute when dressed in diapers.
Cute when clean, but when they're spotty,
You'd look cuter on the potty.

So wake up now. Let's start again.
One day you'll love porcelain!
To the toilet! Are you ready?
Damn! You've plugged it with your teddy!

PAS DE STEW

Here is another poem that immortalizes the parent/child relationship. It is a family connection that Mr. Richardson holds dear to his heart, as he himself is the child of parents. Pas de Stew was written in response to a request for a poem that would honour all the hardworking parents whose ingenuity is taxed from year to year when they have to make yet another costume for yet another dance recital.

March had come in like a lamb, the icicles were dwindling,
The snowbank's high deposits showed the certain signs of swindling.
Wintertime had hit the skids, and spring showed life signs vital:
The robin and the crocus and of course—the spring recital.

The dancers brought the letters home: the tiny terpsichorines
Would soon all don their costumes and across the stage go soaring.
Their teacher, Mrs. Bombardier, was trying something new:
The theme for this year's *soirée* was "A Ballerina Stew"

In other years her dancers had delighted and regaled
Their audience interpreting the classic fairy tales.
Some played elves and princesses, while others played the hedge:
But for the stew they had to dress as gravy, meat, and veg.

All across the city mothers moaned, "I just can't bear it!
How on earth can I transmute my daughter to a carrot?
Her sister's danced for seven years, her interest's more than faddish:
But where can I find patterns for an eggplant or a radish?"

Mrs. Johnson looked aghast and nearly popped her cork
On learning that her Cynthia was cast as "cube of pork",
And likewise did her neighbour, Mrs. Morris, cry with grief,
When Natalie, her daughter, told her "Mama, I'm the beef!"

And oh! But there were mutterings of sundry foul devices
By moms and dads whose kids were cast as turnips, or as spices.
And Mr. Rosen kicked the cat, and nearly kicked the poodle
When he found out his triplets were to play the bed of noodles.

But nonetheless, they buckled down, and did not moan or linger.
They purchased bolts of fabric, and then dusted off the Singer.
Here and there intrepid Dads, and mothers by the score
Cut and stitched and pinned and hemmed and—*sotto voce*—swore.

They fabricated costumes with an amplitude of legroom:
Their offspring were transmogrified from kids to lovely legumes,
While those assigned more meaty roles in their forthcoming festival
Were trimmed of fat, and raised no fears of bypass or cholesterol.

Eventually the great day came. The hall buzzed like an auction,
The families craned their necks to see this stewy dance concoction.
The room went black, the spotlights glowed, the set was all aglimmer,
The onions rushed to centre stage, and primed themselves to simmer.

Their teacher took the tape machine and pressed the proper button,
Expecting that she'd hear the chords that cued the beets and mutton,
Expecting that she'd see prance on the garlic and the Crisco:
But something had gone far awry: the tape was playing disco.

No, this was not the Schubert that her work was based upon,
It wasn't even Mahler, Schumann, Britten, Ives or Brahms.
No, this was Donna Summer flying high on some ingestible,
And not what she'd intended for her savory comestible.

Poor dear Mrs. Bombardier! She stood there stiff and frozen,
She murmured, "Oh, I want to die! Dear Lord, let me be chosen!"
She heard somebody snicker, heard some others start to giggle:
Then on the stage the stew began to giggle and to wiggle.

The onions boogied till they brought a tear to every eye,
The leeks were springing everywhere, the spuds were on the fly.
What might have been disastrous, might have sputtered, coughed, and fizzled,
Was hot as jalepeno. This was stew that really sizzled!

The cubes of beef and pork jumped up, and spattered in the oil,
The triplets dressed as noodles whirled their yellow pasta coils,
Every child looked like a star, not one of them a shy lump:
Bombardier's disaster soon became her greatest triumph.

The parents were ecstatic, and they gave a long ovation.
Now every single dancing class has record registration.
And Mrs. Bombardier has spawned a ritual that tittles:
Vernal dirty dancing done by kids dressed up as victuals.

THE GIFT ETERNAL

One of Mr. Richardson's most applauded poems, this is in fact an adaptation of an earlier prose piece. A gentleman (or in any case, a man) had read Mr. Richardson's essay describing his mother's habit of buying him, each and every Christmas, new underwear. This struck such a resonant chord with the reader that he asked Mr. Richardson to rejig the aforementioned morsel of juvenalia as a poem. We are all the richer for it.

Mother dear, it's time again:
Now the year is on the wane,
Long the nights and dark the days.
Soon you'll trundle to the Bay.
Just like moms across the land
You will have your list in hand,
Wallet ready, poised to buy
Socks and shirts and belts and ties,
Sure as weeks begin with Sundays,
You will buy a score of undies,
You will spend your hard earned coin
So your sons can gird their loins.
Mom, your boys are pushing fifty
And their hair's receding swiftly.
Nonetheless they're still your sons,
Each one blessed with tender buns,
Buns to shield against the weather:
Likewise their equipment nether.
In their thirties and their forties
They acquired autos sporty,
They bought homes and Rolex watches,
But they look to you for gotches.
Sure as ten precedes eleven
Every year you buy pairs seven,
Faithful as an ancient geyser,
Seven pairs! Mom ain't no miser.
Mom, you're kindness, bone and marrow,
But your palette's rather narrow.
Sure as stars come out at night
Mom will always purchase white.

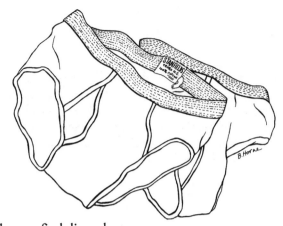

Wilder shades you find discordant.
Do you think them less absorbent?
Do you find them hard to handle,
Think that they might cause a scandal?
Do you think some nurse would fuss,
If your son, stuck by a bus,
To her ward was fast transported
And they found that he disported
Undies that were checked or spotted.
Would they grow distraught, besotted?
Would they cry or come a cropper
If they read "Home of the Whopper"
Written large across his drawers?
Mom—they've seen it all before.
Mom, your sons are middle-aged,
Now's the time to flip the page,
Show them you're a modern parent,
Buy them something quite transparent.
Wean them of their mother's milk,
Buy them satin, buy them silk,
Buy them something rude and cocky,
Fuchsia briefs or flavoured jockeys:
Demonstrate to all your fellows,
Mother can be less than mellow.
Silken shorts for all the kiddos.
For yourself a merry widow!
Do it Mom. Be wild. Be bad,
Next year work on dear old dad.
It's a New Age transformation:
Underwear as Liberation.

MY DAUGHTER, THE DUDE

Let us continue our examination of the filial relationship. This poem was written for Vicki Gabereau, the broadcaster, who made the rather ill-advised decision to take a vacation on a dude ranch. The Poet imagines her sending journal entries back to her mother. On those rare occasions when he is invited to a social gathering, the Poet is almost always asked, "What is Vicki Gabereau really like?" Rest assured, she is not the sort of woman who keeps a journal. Poetic license, then, is here much in evidence.

Dear Mother:

Remember on my birthday, of the year that I turned seven
You gave to me a cowgirl suit. I looked just like Dale Evans.
It launched me on a summer of exhausting western antics,
Of singing 'Happy Trails To You', until I drove you frantic.
And though I fast outgrew the urge to take as my vocation
A life of herding cows and sheep in some far outback station,
At some subconscious level, if you want to know the truth,
I've clung fast to that early aspiration of my youth.
So this year when the time came for my annual *vacances*,
I headed to the dude ranch. It is there I am ensconced.
I'm here with other members of the rooted urban gentry.
Herewith a portrait of the place, made up of journal entries.

Day 1

I got up in the morning to the rooster's raucous crowing:
I didn't think they crowed before a speck of light was showing.
I took out all my brand new gear: the plaid, the boots, the straps,
And then I took my travel iron and flattened out my chaps.
Alas the wrinkles proved themselves recalcitrant and daunting.
The smell as well, I have to tell, was nothing short of haunting.
At breakfast I had hoped to find a loaded, groaning board,
Laden with a hearty feast fit for some Hunnish hoard.
I pelted to the kitchen to load up my breakfast tray:
Happily, I'm rather fond of toast and Special K.

Day 2

Today we went out riding. As we mucked out all the stalls
I realized my brand new boots were several sizes small.
My horse, they said, was kindly, and they called her little Nell:
She proved to be on furlough from some ranch in deepest Hell.
When all the other horses started on their gentle trudge
Nell could not be coaxed to trot, to canter or to budge.
She stood stock still and would not move, but when she saw a stallion
She scudded off towards him like a pirate in a galleon.
I bellowed stop! I hollered halt! She didn't pay me heed. Oh,
Thus did I fall victim to unleashed equine libido.
But here's what finally drove me to take comfort alcoholic:
My legs' brand new geometry: their shape is parabolic.

Day 3

Today we got to take a rope and tie a firm lasso
To snare a straying heifer or a passing buckaroo.
I took my new-made lariat to practise in a spare room
And somehow snagged and brought to earth a small and priceless heirloom.
And then they took us branding and they showed us what to do
I hope you don't get frantic when you see my new tattoo.
It's compact and attractive! There was really nothing to it.
It's situated where my closest friends alone can view it.
Tomorrow there's a rodeo, we'll show off what we've learned.
And when it come to my turn I'll display my scars and burns,
And possibly I'll sing this song: no other song will do.
I'm exhausted. Night night mother. Happy trails to you.

OH DEAR DARLING DAUGHTERS

The observant reader will notice that with this poem, the mother/daughter theme is further explored. A woman requested a poem that would encourage her grown-up daughters to come home and retrieve their goods and chattels.

Oh dear darling daughters, oh fruit of my loins,
How far from the cradle you've roamed!
How often I've pondered the ponderous promise
I made on the day you left home.

How often I've thought of that oath, rashly spoken,
The source of my sorrow and shame:
"Mother," you said, "though our rooms are now vacant,
We hope that you'll leave them the same."

I quickly agreed and a dutiful mother
Should cling to her word till the end.
But frankly, dear daughters, this sordid assortment
Is driving me right 'round the bend.

And though I might wish that our filial friendship
Will deepen and grow through the years,
I shall not forget you, oh dear, darling daughters,
Without all these cheap souvenirs.

So come get your pennants, your pins and your pandas,
Your pictures, your papers, your pumps:
The perilous pile of your paraphernalia
Could fill at least ten city dumps.

Oh, lay claim to Barbie, to Ken and to Skipper,
And likewise to vile Chatty Cathy,
And surely you're ready to take back that teddy
Before the whole mess drives me batty.

Remember the summer you undertook tennis,
Remember the hundred buck racket?
It's stringless and lonely, and dusty and homely,
So honey, come home soon and pack it.

And though I was fond of your various boyfriends
And thought of their love gifts as cute,
They gave them to you—not to me, darling daughters—
So come home and take back your loot.

And while you are at it remember the yearbooks,
And all that you pressed 'twixt their pages.
Take back Nancy Drew, take your saxophone, too,
And assorted rodentia cages.

Oh dear darling daughters, oh fruit of my loins,
I don't mean to cast clouds of gloom.
But come home and clean out your various chambers—
I'm going to rent out your rooms.

OUTSIDE, LOOKIN' IN

Mr. Richardson, who is as cultured as they come, harbours an anomalous passion for country music. This poem, which describes an unhappy mother/daughter relationship, was written with the voice of Patsy Cline in mind. The mother in question is a cat, who was displaced from her home by a conniving kitten.

Fortune is a fickle femme,
Her ways should give you pause.
One day she'll scratch your eyes out
With distinct society claws,
The next she'll share her cream with you,
Then cuff you on the chin:
That's why though I was once inside,
I'm outside lookin' in.

I used to be an inside cat, the planet was my oyster,
I had a velvet cushion in my cozy little cloister,
I had a hundred catnip toys, I had a golden dish,
And two devoted tall ones who would grant my every wish.
And when the stars were shining and the night was thick and calm
I'd go into the barnyard and I'd entertain the toms.
Yes, when the tall ones lay in bed, and when their eyes were shut,
I'd sneak out through the window and I'd act the perfect slut.
I'd use them up and toss them out until the break of day,
Then slip inside and dream sweet dreams of wee ones on the way.
Oh, this was how I lived my life! Oh, how I loved my work!
But then the kitten came along who wiped away my smirk.

Fortune is a fickle femme,
Her ways should give you pause.
One day she'll scratch your eyes out
With distinct society claws,
The next she'll share her cream with you,
Then cuff you on the chin:
That's why though I was once inside,
I'm outside lookin' in.

At first she showed no outward sign of how she'd turn my luck,
Just like her seven siblings all she did was snooze and suck.
I saw no sign or portent that she'd make me get the boot:
Kittens, just like firemen, are always cute, cute, cute.
But as the weeks turned into months I saw she had her wiles,
She had a winsome simper, and insinuating smile.
Her littermates were sent outside as soon as they were weaned,
But she contrived to stay behind and stimulate my spleen.
I tolerated her at first, I tried hard not to mind,
But concentrated cuteness is a pain in the behind.
One day we had a little chat, I used no hidden code:
"Beat it bitch," I whispered, and she hit the dusty road.

Fortune is a fickle femme,
Her ways should give you pause.
One day she'll scratch your eyes out
With distinct society claws,
The next she'll share her cream with you,
Then cuff you on the chin:
That's why though I was once inside,
I'm outside lookin' in.

The next three months were paradise. My kingdom was my own.
I strolled along the counter singing songs like "Home sweet home".
From time to time I caught a mouse or shrew or such as that.
What a feline fool I was to fail to smell a rat!
One day the tall ones came inside, one bearing in his arms
The object of my loathing. She was turning on the charm.
I hissed. I spit. I arched. In short, began a full scale pout.
Summarily they picked me up, and rudely put me out.
And now the little trollop eats my tuna from my bowl,
She sits upon my cushion and my heart is black as coal.
"How are the mighty fallen" has become my favourite line.
But I've got tricks she's never seen and vengeance will be mine.

Fortune is a fickle femme,
Her ways should give you pause.
One day she'll scratch your eyes out
With distinct society claws,
The next she'll share her cream with you,
Then cuff you on the chin:
That's why though I was once inside,
I'm outside lookin' in.

INSIDE, LOOKIN' OUT

The Bard often receives requests for poems about cats. He is an ardent catophile, and is happy to comply. In this poem, he endeavours to answer the great imponderable: what do cats get up to when we are out of the house?

Each morning when you go to work, you bid the cats "so long",
And kiss their furry noggins while they croon their plaintive song,
"Don't go, don't go," they seem to plead with every heartfelt mew.
Oh, it would split your heart atwain to hear their purred "Adieu!"

"Now who's a noisy cat?" you say, "Now why should pussy pout?
I've filled your bowl with crunchies and I've cleaned your litter out.
You've got your ball to play with, and you've got a rubber mouse!"
You say a final toodleoo, and then you leave the house.

The cats watch from the window as you hurry down the street,
They look like feline angels: pure of heart, refined, discreet.
Until you turn the corner they comport themselves like nuns:
But then it's, "See ya sucker! We is gonna have some fun!"

The first thing that your kittens do is start to work the phones.
They call up all their friends and say, "Dig this. We're home alone!
The two legged wonder's gone to work. Hot dog! Another chance
To claw the chairs to ribbons and to chew her favourite plants.

We'll scoop up sandy litter and then strew it on the bed!
Come on by," they tell their pals, "and you can help us shed!"
And now they've lit a smouldering fuse! They're sitting on a bomb!
The kitty grapevine spreads the word to every randy tom.

Soon party hearty cats drop in, intent upon a bender:
They come with cream and catnip and instructions for the blender.
They like their cocktails potent, and they like their music wild,
"The Doggy in the Window" rends them rabid, raging, riled.

They rent alarming videos, and make a dreadful din
Yelling "Slut!" at Lassie and insulting Rin Tin Tin.
And though you cannot see them it is more than sure and certain
They strap on tiny crampons and ascend the kitchen curtains.

And some play spin the bottle, while a few seek rougher trade.
Yours may well be neutered, but not all of them are spayed.
If teddy bears should stumble in, I'd wager that they'd faint
To see this Bacchanalia, for a picnic, boys, it ain't.

They're wolves inside the henhouse, they're the black sheep in the fold:
There's more to tell, but darling, it would make your blood run cold.
The moment that the clock strikes four, the neighbour cats disperse.
Your own begin to sweep and mop and squirrel away the worst.

At five o'clock, when you come in, they greet you in the hall,
To wind themselves between your legs and fawn and purr and call.
"Did kitty miss me then?" you ask, and "Who's my hungry puss?"
Never have you heard their *sotto voce* whisper, "Wuss!"

Though cats will let you cuddle them and deign to share your bed,
And ride upon your shoulders and repose upon your head,
They'll never share their secret lives. They spend their days half-masked:
Sorry for the brutal truth. But after all, you asked.

HE SCOOPS TO CONQUER

The Poet is as fond of dogs as he is of cats. This poem was requested by a dog owner whose life was made miserable by a boorish neighbour. The Poet knows that boorishness is almost always the province of bipeds, and was pleased to take the dog's side. An investigation to discover the truth was deemed wholly unnecessary. This is poetry, after all.

All hail the loving puppy dog,
A pal who has no peer!
When days become a tired slog
A vile morass, a foul bog,
A tangled mess of rusted cogs,
Take heart! For doggy's near!

I love my trusted, furry chum,
My quadrupedal mate:
If I am sad and tired and glum,
Look longingly at gin and rum,
And zero seems life's total sum
Sweet doggy sets me straight.

Puppy makes me goo and coo
Ensuring that I thrive:
Nothing would I rather do
Than skip with doggy to the loo,
Those plastic bags replete with poo
Sure gladden both our lives.

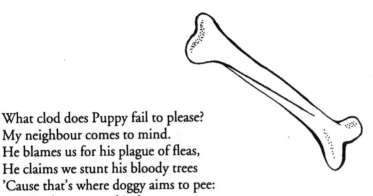

What clod does Puppy fail to please?
My neighbour comes to mind.
He blames us for his plague of fleas,
He claims we stunt his bloody trees
'Cause that's where doggy aims to pee:
Some jerks are so unkind.

My neighbour is a perfect lout,
He rides a Harley D.
His friends come by and shriek and shout
They gun their bikes and tear about,
That they are brutes there's little doubt
It's plain as plain can be.

Though doggy's innocent and sweet
It's sometimes hard to tell:
She can be rather indiscreet,
As when, for instance, as a treat
She stole my neighbour's boot to eat
He didn't take it well.

He found the boot and fast surmised
The tooth marks weren't his own.
He bellowed out his rude surprise
I heard his anguished "why oh why?"
And then his footfalls, quick and spry:
He sprinted to my home.

Just like the big bad wolf he roared,
All windy and tattooed,
Shouting, "Open up this door!"
Yelling what he had in store,
Making threats of blood and gore,
My goodness but he's rude!

It's gone on now for several hours:
He's still out on the stoop,
With his face on perma-glower,
Shouting there while we two cower
Me and puppy in the shower,
Waiting till he's pooped.

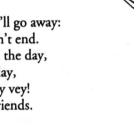

In time's good course he'll go away:
Our torture though, won't end.
From now on we'll shun the day,
Just go out at night to play,
Fearing that he might, oy vey!
Come back with some friends.

I fear that we might have to leave:
We might be safer gone.
The prospect makes me feel aggrieved,
Bitter too, and more than peeved.
So pup, be sure before we leave
To go and foul his lawn.

You loving naughty puppy dog,
You pal who has no peer!
Though days may seem a tired slog
A vile morass, a foul bog,
A tangled mess of rusted cogs:
Praise Heaven, puppy's near!

THE RAPE OF THE LOCKS

The Poet Laureate is a victim of Male Pattern Baldness. He is very sensitive about it. He knows that a barber must pay great heed to the few strands that cling to the skulls of those who live with MPB. Most stylists, though, are criminally cavalier and dismissive. The Poet poured his heart and soul into this poem to commemorate a bad haircut given someone without much hair to cut.

Once a month I make a trek of several city blocks
To visit Nick, my barber, and entrust to him my locks.
Nick pulls out his blade and shears and tends my thinning fleece
And tells me of his boyhood in his native country, Greece.
Mrs. Nick works in the back, and sometimes Nick confesses
His minor infidelities while trussing up my tresses.
It's been like this for several years: our two souls are well-tuned.
I pay him ten bucks, tip him two, and say, "I'll see you soon."

In the years preceding Nick, I used to patronize
Some chic salon that catered to the whims of hirsute guys
With Samson-like long shocks of hair cascading from their skulls.
But oh alas, the high-paid staff all found me rather dull,
They'd snarl when I came in the door, and quickly start kvetching:
They'd argue over what poor sod would have to patch my thatching.
And though they'd charge me thirty bucks to try their latest tricks
My scalp still showed. So now I give myself to Nick.

On Saturday I trundled off to get my monthly trimming
And gripe again with Nick about the way my hair is thinning.
But when I reached his shop I only found an empty chair.
Mrs. Nick came from the back. "Nicky, he not there.
Nicky he go back to Greece, his father not so good."
I made the kind of tut-tut sounds that any of us would.
Respectfully, I bowed my head, I tried to sympathize:
The sun bounced off my bald spot and she shielded her eyes.

She said to me, "You have a seat. His cousin coming by.
He cut hair good." I figured that I'd give the guy a try,
Assuming, as I did, that Nicky's talents were familial
And that I'd find his cousin charming, talented, convivial.
Oh what a fool I was to place such credence in genetics!
Now I've been had, I'm sad, I'm mad! I am, in short, splenetic.
It turned out Nicky's cousin—who was aptly named Orestes—
Was Nicky's polar opposite: callous, cold, and testy.

"How ya want it cut?" he snarled, directly he came in.
"Just a bit off here and there, you know: a tidy trim,"
I said, a tiny bit alarmed to hear Orestes' gnashing.
He held my head as though it were a melon, ripe for smashing.
"Ya wanna trim, ya get a trim," he muttered, and then leering,
Took his weapon and began a kind of wholesale shearing.
He started at the neck line and proceeded to the crown,
He raked his vicious razor up my skull again, then down.

It seemed to me his strategy, while making one swift pass
Was not unlike the one one uses when one cuts the grass.
Within thirty seconds, what had been on top was gone:
I would have been impressed had he been working on my lawn.
Without exaggeration, and without the risk of perjury
I'll tell you that I looked prepared for hasty neurosurgery.
Orestes waxed nostalgic, and proclaimed in tones all smarmy:
"That was how I cut 'em back when I was in the army."

And then to finally prove to me that I was out of luck,
I asked "What do I owe you?" And he told me "Twenty bucks."
My hair will one day sprout again, will rise up from the rubble,
Already I detect it stirring, there amidst the stubble.
I know that Nick will come back soon. It gives my soul a lift
To think of how on his return I'll bring my Greek a gift:
A sign to hang up in his shop, whose point is far from moot:
A sign that reads: "Nick's Barber Shop. Accept no substitute."

AUTOMAD

Mr. Richardson is fascinated by metamorphosis and transformation. He was most intrigued by a letter, from Edmonton, describing the Jekyll and Hyde shift in temperament that came over a woman called Evelyn when, at the age of 36, she finally acquired a driver's license.

I have a friend called Evelyn, refinement's distillation:
Discreet and sweet, she'd never bleat a word like constipation,
You might invite this true delight to any high flown luncheon
And know that she would not say "pee" or mention other functions.
She'd never wheeze or cough or sneeze or snort or sniff or whinny,
It wouldn't do to mention Pooh, not even charming Winnie.

Evelyn was pure, for sure, and disinclined to sin:
She'd never break a heart or vase. She'd never broken wind .
As near as anybody knew she'd never belched or drooled:
And even when she perched on one she would not utter "stool".
She wasn't really rigid or retentive you-know-where,
She simply bought what she was taught: the body isn't there.

Sweet Evelyn, at 36, had never learned to drive:
She claimed it made her nervous, and she feared she might get hives.
And Evelyn, sweet Evelyn, refinement's own quintessence
Could not abide the thought of hives or some such foul excrescence.
I'm not sure what possessed her then, to one day lift the phone,
And call a local driving school and then go get a loan.

She purchased a Toyota, which was promptly christened Kermit.
A green machine, a clean machine: she swiftly got her permit.
She came to call soon afterwards to take me for a spin,
She opened up the pristine door. I stepped demurely in.
But hardly had we started out upon our pleasant ride
When I perceived that Evelyn had turned to Mrs. Hyde.

I'd never heard sweet Evelyn raise so much as a squeal,
But something foul possessed her when she sat behind the wheel.
She'd lived in her pristine cocoon, but now she'd wings to show:
A Metamorphosis you'd find in Kafka, or in Poe.
Evelyn, sweet Evelyn, who'd never, ever cuss,
Rolled her window down and hurled invectives at a bus:

"Get off the road you son of a bitch!" And then, good Lord! She spit,
And said a monosyllable that wasn't twit or nit.
"Park that thing or drive it!" she assailed a passing truck,
And uttered then another word that wasn't luck or buck.
"Hey buddy! Where'd you learn to drive?" became her frequent call.
"Cut me off again," she yelled," and I'll cut off your ___!" All

That I remember from our drive around the town
Was that whenever Evelyn would roll her window down
It wasn't to admire the view or to enjoy the air,
Or to release a bumblebee, but just to curse and swear.
The last time that I had seen her she would blush to mention bowels,
And now a strange scatology informed her every howl.

She filled the air around her with her noxious, loud emissions:
But straight away she stopped the car and turned off the ignition
She once again became the dame refinement smiled upon,
Evelyn, who never belched, or had to use the john.
Oh what a lingering mystery! That one so good and pure
Could turn into a maniac while driving a *voiture.*

Oh how bizarre that just a car could make her blow a gasket,
This girl so rare who dared not swear from cradle unto casket.
See her at a party and you'll think she's on the level,
See her on the highway and you'll think you've met the devil.
Her life on foot's pedestrian. With wheels her life's a gas.
At 36, she's learned new tricks. She's set to kick some ass.

A STATISTICAL IMPROBABILITY

Mr. Richardson often receives requests for poems to mark the anniversary celebrations of couples who have endured one another for many years. This is his "one size fits all" ode. The Bard admires this kind of longevity, as he himself has a rather spotty record when it comes to Relationship Maintenance. Now, he confines his activities to the odd weekend here and there, and the occasional phone call to a 1-900 number somewhere in New York.

Oh, Happy Anniversary! Hurrah! Congratulations!
Another year has come and gone, and still you're man and wife!
You've neither one thrown in the towel, nor turned to strangulation,
You took like ducks to water to the state of wedded life.

You made it through the harried years of puking, squalling babies,
The years of vacant bank accounts, the jobs you called the pits,
You didn't cave at seven years, although you itched like scabies,
You've stuck it out for all this time and never called it quits

Your family and your friends have all assembled here to toast you.
They wonder how you've managed it. They ask, "What do you do
To keep your marriage young and fresh?" And though you never boast, you
Look around and see you're a minority of two.

There's Marla, here from Montreal without her husband Harold.
Harold followed Jack who followed Sam whom no one liked.
Sam came after Claude, who followed in the wake of Gerald,
Now absent Harold's being dumped for Gerald's brother, Mike.

Brian came with Marilyn, who thinks all's hunkydory,
But one suspects the happy spouse will change her cheery tune
When Marilyn unravels Brian's frayed and tattered stories
And learns about his other wives, in Sooke and Saskatoon.

Clara left her husband, Ned, and changed her name to Parsley,
Then joined a women's commune where she's fondly known as Pip.
Now she just wears Birkenstocks and keeps her hair cut sparsely
And asks, "Is it organic?" when she's offered chips and dip.

Sally and her second spouse have got twelve kids between them:
The oldest one, at 26, has moved back home to stay.
The youngest two are twins, and Sally's managed just to wean them,
And now at 44, she finds she's in the family way.

Your daughter's husband's ex comes with her live-in lover, Bobby.
Your niece, 18, presents her husband: this is number three.
It seems a tad excessive, but a girl should have a hobby:
If hers is having weddings—well, what's that to you or me?

Everybody lifts a glass, expressing admiration:
You stand there, hand in hand, as you have often stood before,
Knowing that in constancy you've found your satiation,
Happy in the knowledge that you'll still have many more.

MARPIES

An acronym coined by the requester of this poem, who numbers herself among the ever-growing legion of city dwellers who, in mid-life, flee the urban scene for Arcadia. She wrote to Mr. Richardson, describing the gunning down of some predator (possibly a skunk) who had the temerity to invade the hen house. Middle-Aged Rural People everywhere requested copies of this poem when it was first broadcast.

Oh let the fire burn out my love, prod not the glowing coal,
Feed not the starving flame more beech or pine!
Life is but a storm-tossed sea, this hour's a welcome shoal:
You're middle-aged, you're rural, and you're mine!

The room is dark, the cocoa's drained, the almanac's been read,
We've listened to *The Journal's* high-priced panel.
Like all good Marpies we must take our two selves off to bed,
And don our stylish nightgowns made of flannel.

And nestled 'neath the quilt we'll hear the cats content and purring,
We'll hear our brutish neighbour's pick-up gunning.
Perhaps beneath the flannel we might feel a pleasant stirring:
For after all, it's spring! The sap is running.

And through the meadow, through the wood, and through the thorny copse,
The time is done for droning winter's dirges!
Everything that creeps or crawls, that swims or slinks or hops,
Is singing hymns to nature's baser urges.

And shall we join them in that choir, take part in their devotions,
This pantheistic raising of the dickens?
We should indeed, but first let's see what's causing the commotion
Within the spacious condo of the chickens.

Oh father grab your blunderbuss, and mother seize your boots,
And hasten out to end the vermin's spree!
The great horned owl observing us declares that it's a hoot!
Now here's a bird's eye view of what he sees:

A pair of flustered Marpies in assorted, mismatched garments,
Scared as hell, and mad enough to spit,
Peering through the dark for some marauding, filthy varmint,
Swearing low, and slogging slow through grit.

Their winter-whitened legs reveal a universe of goose-flesh,
They vow to have the foul intruder's hide.
They stumble to the hen house and discover that some loose mesh
Let the creature easily inside.

Oh mother, shine your steady beam! Oh father, draw your bead!
Oh take a breath, and steel yourselves, and fire!
The shot is heard around the world. The owl in his tree
Shrieks out the news of someone who's expired.

We two bedraggled Marpies calm the clucking, ruffled tenants.
It's hours before their garbled gossip dies.
If they played God, they'd see the sod perform some painful penance,
And then take turns at pecking out his eyes.

When peace has come again at last and everyone is settled,
We stumble to the house as in a dream,
And pause en route to bed to toast our tested Marpie mettle
By raising up a glass of Irish Cream.

Thus fortified, we'll go again and nestle in our cot,
We'll whisper soft the oft repeated line
That sums up all the happiness our kind of life has brought:
You're middle-aged, you're rural and you're mine.

BRUCE THE MOOSE

Another poem in which Mr. Richardson makes hay with an accident involving firearms. A forest ranger from Delta, B.C. wrote asking for a poem based on a sordid event from his own past. In order to impress "a couple of chicks" who had expressed a fondness for hairy chests, the ranger and one of his buddies attached the pelt of a recently deceased moose to their midsections. Much hilarity ensued. Here, the Poet indulges himself (and us) in an exercise in role reversal.

Bruce the Moose had honed his body at the forest gym:
A striking figure, handsome, tall, possessed
Of stunning features. One so rarely sees the likes of him:
The chiselled profile, antlers, snout and chest.

A chest made for medallions, it was thick with fecund fur,
A chest to show off in the spring cotillion,
A chest that on a public beach would generate a stir,
A chest that one might even call Sicilian.

A chest distinguished, furthermore, by mountainous pectorals,
Massive moosles rippled through his flesh.
When Bruce was loose the lady moose would bicker, scrap and quarrel:
But Marie-Claire, alas, was not impressed.

Marie-Claire, whom Bruce adored, was native to Quebec,
And how she wandered here no one can tell:
It's certain though that as she made the long cross-country trek
All dressed in puce, a dozen bull-moose fell.

And Brucie fell the hardest, almost cracking with the strain.
His brain turned soft, like fruit gone overripe.
Whenever he saw Marie-Claire he'd bellow like a train,
But Marie-Claire would sniff, "You're not my type!

Your chest is far too hairy. You have too much chevelure,
Your hormones are too much out of control.
That excess of testosterone has made you less than pure,
You're too much taken by your bullmoose role.

I want a moose whose chest is hairless, like a boiled peach,
With skin that's softer than an angel's sigh.
And Bruce, in truth, that chest appears so far out of your reach
I can't see any hope. *Alors*—bye-bye!"

How desolate was Bruce the Moose! He wandered through the woods,
His Casanova eye had lost it's twinkle!
He wondered how he'd ever get depilatory goods:
The road was rocky for this sad Bullwinkle.

He wandered high, he wandered low, he wandered without reason,
His only thought was love for Marie-Claire.
The weeks turned into months, till one day hunters were in season,
And Bruce found one who'd stumbled on a snare.

"Poor fellow," muttered Bruce, as he surveyed the fallen lad
Who wore a Bluejays cap and downy vest,
And Bruce the moose could see that underneath his shirt of plaid
The hunter had a smooth and hairless chest.

In Bruce's brain the penny dropped. He said, "Ah, ma cherie!
At last I've found a way that I might kiss you."
He rooted round the carcass on his knobby, moosey knees,
And found the hunter's knife—Swiss Army issue.

Now you can well imagine what transpired on that day:
I won't disclose each sad and sordid thing.
I shall not drop a ton of bricks. It is enough to say
It looked like something out of Stephen King.

The next day lovely Marie-Claire heard someone at her door.
"Who's there?" she trilled, "Attends! J'arrive toute de suite!
I hope it's someone nice and not some macho, hirsute bore
Who hopes to come and sweep me off my feet."

She opened up the door, and there stood Bruce all rearranged.
"Mon dieu!" she said, "Mon dieu! I am impressed!
I never thought I'd see the day that Bruce the Moose would change!
But holy moly what a gorgeous chest!"

"Oh la la!" said Marie-Claire, and, "Oh la la" again,
And "Oh la la la la la la" once more.
"Oh la la la la la la la la!" was her refrain
The instant she dragged Brucie through the door.

This was several years ago. The two are joyous yet:
They thank their lucky stars that they've been blessed
With mortgage, house and garden and a couple of moosettes
And nothing to get off their happy chests.

RENDERING TO CAESAR

An Alberta woman contacted the self-appointed Poet Laureate to report that her husband was, for the very first time, trying to fill out an income tax form. Time and time again he did this, and always with vastly differing results. The Bard was very sympathetic to this dilemma, as he himself is among the tax challenged.

Payday rolls 'round twice a month, and every second week
Pecuniary circumstances seem a tad less bleak.
You scamper down to get your cheque and buss the parole clerk
And recollect the reason why you come each day to work.
A general euphoria comes o'er you like a dove:
You feel inclined to see mankind in terms of grace and love.
You think of how your near-to-zero balance in the bank
Will hit the triple digit mark, and offer hymns of thanks.
You know you cannot stow the dough. You've creditors in spades,
But still no bliss can equal this—the moment one is paid.
The cheque is in the envelope. Oh ecstasy lies close!
You wrest it from its hiding place, survey the net and gross.
And happiness slipslides away, like water off a duck:
You see the huge discrepancy and think the whole thing sucks.
The size of those deductions every payday makes you blue.
You've rendered unto Caesar more than any Caesar's due.
And though they say it goes to pay to keep the country strong,
You nonetheless are unimpressed and think somehow it's wrong
To tax and tax the middle class to serve the nation's needs:
The clods on top can slice and chop but we're the ones who bleed.
Every payday it's the same—you start out with a smile
That rapidly evaporates in fits of pique and bile.
You rend your garments, gnash your teeth and curse the dreadful news:
But all this pales to nothingness when income tax falls due.

It's insult heaped on injury. Their sharp rapacious horns
Gouge you all the goddamn year, and then they send you forms
That seem devised to make one's eyes grow bleary with the strain
Of trying to decipher them again and then again.
You've got a shoebox filled with slips—T4s and T4As,
And all the other chits and chips they send so you can play
This convoluted poker game that no one understands,
That makes you feel emasculated, gelded, and unmanned.
The labyrinthine set of rules makes mincemeat of the brain:
Take so much off for every child, so much for loss or gain,
Add this if you are married, figure interest, bonds and stocks:
A single error guarantees a cell with umpteen locks.
You answer all the pertinents, you add, subtract, divide,
And when you've reached the bottom line, and scrupulously tried
To tell the truth and just the truth you find you're in arrears:
You owe them thirty thousand bucks. Your cheeks are damp with tears,
But this is surely incorrect. It's more than what you earned.
You start again, and feel a sickly welling of concern
At seeing they owe you as much. Your shrieking tears the air,
You rip and shred the bloody form, you ululate and swear.
You ask the Lord why you were born, and rue the very day,
And then pick up the telephone and call a CGA.
They've got you where they want you, by the curlies and the shorts,
So let me say by way of terminating this report:
The bastards who inflict this pain deserve to go to hell.
The devil take the taxman then. I hope he roasts him well.

HAVE GUMS, WILL TRAVEL

This is one of a series of customized curses that Mr. Richardson has written for Canadians who have a serious bone to pick. This one was commissioned by a man in Montreal who was in a stylish restaurant and who watched, with grotesque fascination, someone at a neighbouring table floss her teeth. This poem is a spirited imprecation directed against all those who would perform acts of private hygiene in public places. That the need for such a poem exists makes one wonder if it's worthwhile going on.

The citizen has duties he's required to perform,
And some of these exact a public forum:
The voting booth, the picket line, and aiding the forlorn
Suggest a certain conduct and decorum.
And then there are hygienic acts, quotidian and trite,
The brushing and the flossing and the rest
That properly should be performed when one is out of sight:
To keep such functions private's for the best.

In fact when I espy a clod who's in the public eye
Engaged in something quintessentially private,
My bile and blood begin to boil, the curses start to fly:
Forthwith the imprecations I've arrived at.
To all you thoughtless twits who in a restaurant or a queue
Take a length of floss and, making passes
Through your teeth, anoint the room with toothy residue,
And leave your spots on other people's glasses:

To you I wish a legacy of lacerated gums,
And dentures well before the age of thirty,
I wish on you a root canal for every time you strum
Your teeth in public. Dirty! Dirty! Dirty!
And those of you who mount the bus, and then without a blush,
Reach deeply in your pocket or your purse,
Extract therefrom a comb, or else, perhaps, a ratty brush:
On you I wish another custom curse:

B. Horne

For all the stray and sordid strands that from your scalp you've culled,
For all the flakes that fall in fulsome flurry,
And other vile excrescences you've lifted from your skull,
I send you straight to hell, and in a hurry.
And gentlemen who use the gym, and wander to the sauna,
And think that it's the perfect place to shave,
Who sit about its steamy climes like razor-wielding bwanas,
You, I say, are vagabonds and knaves.

So, woe upon your houses and may woe befall you soon!
When next you stoop to public depilation,
I hope you leave the sauna limp and wrinkled as a prune,
Bedecked with nicks and serious abrasions.
And you who chew with open mouths and show what therein lurks,
Who drive with index fingers stuck up noses:
Whose public demonstrations place you in the ranks of jerks,
I wish a life not redolent of roses.

And now that I've chastised you all, and labelled you as sinners,
Who live in dire need of absolution,
I'll take my leave. My teeth are strung with strands of recent dinners,
I've got to go and undertake ablutions.
I'll floss away in private, and I'll Q-tip out my ears,
I'll lock the door and polish my enamel.
Private acts accomplished, I'll go work on my career:
Turning into God's most perfect mammal.

THE STROKE OF MIDNIGHT

Another of the Poet's jibes at those who breach the bounds of good taste. His victims, in this case, are enthusiastic kissers on New Year's Eve.

Quelle joie! Another New Year's Eve!
Oh what a happy time!
I love those off-key choruses
Of tunes like Auld Lang Syne,
I love the merry pealing bells,
And burgeoning buffets,
And all the other symbols
That betoken New Years Day.
I love the toys for making noise,
The whistles and the hats,
The crackers and the canapes
And resolutions that
Are broken soon as they are made,
And vanish like the wind,
The boozy-breathed atoning
For the sins that we have sinned.

There's just one single ritual
That frankly I abhor,
That makes me scurry for my coat
And hurry out the door,
That makes me deftly disappear,
And join up with the missing:
The ritual of which I speak
Is that of New Year's kissing.

Oh! Yuck and blech and gag and puke!
I hasten to take cover
When twelve bells peal and all those mouths
Begin to purse and hover.
I loath strange mouths at midnight,
All that sucky face collusion
And now I'll read my catalogue
Of lips and their intrusions.

The lips that want to kiss your cheek,
The lips that aim for lips,
The lips all smeared with pesto
Or besmirched with garlic dips.
The kisser who believes a grope
Will label him a mensch,
The ones who smooch and probe as though
They thought that you were French,
The ones who clench you to their chests
As though in mid thrombosis,
The ones whose mouths are full of mints,
The ones with halitosis,
The ones whose lips are chapped and raw,
The ones whose lips are greasy,
Whose lips are flaked with filo,
And who smell distinctly cheesy.

Oh I could go on but I won't.
You'll sense that I'm no floozy.
At midnight you will find me,
Fully clothed in the jacuzzi.

A GIFT OF COASTERS

The Poet was contacted by a fellow refugee from Winnipeg. He had experienced the all-too common phenomenon of being set upon by his extended family at Christmas time: a great herd of Prairie people, panting after a temperate coastal Yule. The poem tells it all.

My family lives in Winnipeg, and I live on the coast.
The last time that I saw them all I volunteered to host
A Christmas in Vancouver. "Come on out, we'll all be jolly!
We'll cook a goose and trim a tree and deck the halls with holly!
Why wallow through the drifting snow? Come scamper through the rain!"
On Christmas Eve they called my bluff. All fifty seven came.

"Hello!" they gaily carolled as they thundered through the door.
Fifty-seven—some of whom I'd never seen before:
Siblings and their spouses and a swarm of second cousins:
And all of them with offspring. There were babies by the dozen.
Nieces, nephews, infants: squallin', bawlin' and bewilderin'.
And now I know just what it means to suffer all the children.

Take Jimmy for an instance. He's my cousin's tiny tyke.
You should have heard him chuckle when he got that brand new bike.
His little sister Marnie, when she saw it made a dare
That Jimmy wouldn't ride his bike straight down the basement stairs.
He lifted up his little bum and swung the bike beneath.
Now all he wants next Christmas are his missing two front teeth.

And what of cousin Ruthie's lad? The little one called Jason.
When he grows up he wants to be a plumber or a mason.
Or so I guess. He plugged the toilet with my granny's hat,
Then tried to make a plunger of Imelda—that's my cat.
And when the cat resisted little Jason's cunning trick,
He took apart my bookcase and then beaned her with a brick.

Of course there's always Nephew Ned, the son of brother Jack,
Who hammered on the bedroom door when I was in the sack—
Trying to take a tiny nap, like grownups sometimes do.
"Can I come in?" my nephew whined. "I think I've got the flu."
He marched right in. "Go find your dad," said I to little Ned.
And so he did but not before he threw up on the bed.

And Ashley got the measles, and Lucinda got the mumps,
And their second cousin, Harvey, started sprouting tiny bumps.
"Chicken pox," the doctor said, "You've had it, I suppose."
I hadn't though. My body now, from head to trunk to toes
Is covered by these itching blots. They've colonized my skin.
I look like Job. My patience though, is running pretty thin.

Tomorrow, when they've gone away, I'll pour a potent potion,
And swill it down while on my spots I rub a soothing lotion.
I'll put on New Year's music—Guy Lombardo's Auld Lang Syne.
And next year when they call to say, "We're coming," I'll say, "Fine.
The towels are in the closet and the key's beneath the stoop.
And me, I'm in Hawaii. Toodleoo! I've flown the coop."

APPLIANCE RELIANCE

A physician, also in Vancouver, wrote to say that he was in love with a woman who actually wept when she bought, or received as gifts, small appliances. Mr. Richardson does not make these things up. People seek him out to tell him such news. At times, it is more than he can bear. The doctor's tale was so poignant that the Poet could do nothing but cast it as a country song. Tammy Wynette, this one has your name on it.

Oh darling, how could I forget that Christmas 'neath the tree
When you unwrapped my gift to you: a spanking new TV!
I'd feared you'd think it uninspired, insipid and moronic,
But through your trembling lips I heard, "My God! A Panasonic!
It's just the thing I wanted! Oh ! However did you know?"
And then you let the floodgates down, and how the teardrops flowed!
And all throughout that Christmas day, you issued tiny cries:
Your love for small appliances sure took me by surprise.

Chorus:

Your love's the vegematic that has sliced and diced my heart,
Without you here beside me, my whole world would fall apart,
And if someday you leave me, I'll go on a big bad bender:
If love's a vegematic, well then honey, you're the blender.

All my friends and relatives agree that you're a doll:
Of course, they haven't been with us while visiting a mall.
Just last night in Metrotown you left a teary trail,
And all because you found a store with microwaves on sale.
You blubbered as you picked it out: your make-up was a mess.
You blubbered as you charged it to American Express.
Your sobbing as we drove it home was nothing like the din
That poured out like a tempest when we finally plugged it in.

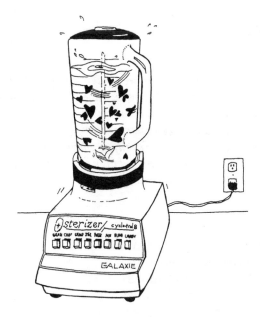

Chorus:

Your love's the vegematic that has sliced and diced my heart,
Without you here beside me, my whole world would fall apart,
And if someday you leave me, I'll go on a big bad bender:
If love's a vegematic, well then honey, you're the blender.

Doubtless there are theories in psychology or science
That might explain the way you act when buying an appliance.
Perhaps in the delivery room you met with a disaster
And bonded not with Mama, but to Hoover, or Mixmaster.
But all I know for sure is this: the tears are sure to start
When you acquire a VCR or else a Cuisinart.
And if some day you say my love alone can't take you higher,
We'll simply go out shopping for a washer or a dryer.

Chorus:

Your love's the vegematic that has sliced and diced my heart,
Without you here beside me, my whole world would fall apart,
And if someday you leave me, I'll go on a big bad bender:
If love's a vegematic, well then honey, you're the blender.

MARMALADE: THE CONTEST

Another verse about preserves, and yet another request originating from Vancouver: a city populated with poetry lovers. A couple and their friends have a marmalade-making contest each year. They started out with a strict definition of marmalade. But as the years progressed, contestants tried to push back the boundaries by preparing orange-based condiments that were leagues removed from the old Scots favourite. Finally, someone blew the whistle, and a wholesale retrenching took place. The Poet was invited to judge the contest, a task he happily undertook. The memory of sampling more than a dozen different marmalades, one after another, still sets his teeth on edge.

It's February one again. Its eight and twenty days
Are brutish, short and nasty, and the winter sun's weak rays
Shake their ineffectual fists, unable to take hold
And drive away the lurking, omnipresent, churlish cold.
All through the month, foul, frigid fronts will glower and absorb
The greetings telegraphed to earth by our beleaguered orb.

 But though old Sol might quake and fall at winter's frosty will
We have a tiny substitute that's native to Seville:
A little sun that warms us on the darkest, bleakest day!
It turns up every winter in the bins at IGA.
No cold, however obdurate, could rob it of its force.
And what's this thing of which I sing? The orange! The orange, of course!

Oh priceless loot! You sun-like fruit, you willingly have lent
Your sour life in sacrifice to make our condiments.
You left the rainy plains of Spain and travelled to our coast.
You let us boil you to a pulp and spread you on our toast.
Heroic orange of Seville, in your Iberian glade
You gladly grow so we might know the thrill of marmalade!

Some years ago a group of friends agreed to have a *fête*.
They'd make and sample marmalades. Who made the best would get
A trophy, kindly kudos, and an hour in the sun
Of general approbation. Everyone had so much fun
That next year they assembled, and the next and next year too,
And the marmalade got better, and the competition grew.

When this was born the friends had sworn to ethically abjure
The use of sundry additives. "Let's keep the product pure.
Let's vow that when we try to make the quintessential spread,
We'll just use sugar, water, oranges, and—of course—our heads.
We will not stoop to opiates, like spices, herbs, or liquor.
Marmalade is marmalade. We needn't make it slicker."

But man's a fallen creature, woman equally terrestrial.
We cave inevitably in to urges base and bestial.
It makes me glum to say these chums were seized by such ambition
That they neglected to respect their charter's first conditions.
So they might win they turned to sin and shed their fine convictions,
And schemingly ensconced themselves within their gleaming kitchens.

The devil stood beside them then. They promised they would trade
Their very souls if they could win with this year's marmalade.
And so it happened on that Mephistophelean day
That someone doped their product with a drop of Grand Marnier,
And someone thought a pinch of clove would be just fine and dandy,
And likewise they tried Cointreau, sticks of cinnamon, and brandy.

And someone plied the judges with a mighty whack of graft.
Greed made them blind. "The trophy's mine!" each villainously laughed.
But good will out, there is no doubt. One pure soul cried *"J'accuse!"*
Blowing thus the cover of this marmalade abuse.
He soundly urged a general purge and started a commission
Which dragged from the competitors their scarlet-cheeked admissions.

They'd blush and shrug and talk of drugs, corruption, and coercion,
They told of sticky steroids and their terrible insertions.
When all was cleanly swept the friends wept buckets and repented,
And rued the day that marmalade had ever been invented.
So learn from their example, every sire and every dame:
The day you mess with marmalade, you'll end up in a jam.

THE TEUTONIC PLAGUE

A North Vancouver woman told of a picnic in an alpine meadow that evolved into one of those glorious outdoor sessions of afternoon lovemaking. Alas, a group of camera-toting German tourists stumbled upon their lovenest, and proved themselves less than discreet. The Poet is astonished, as always, at the things people will reveal about themsleves.

At last! A sunny weekend in this summer of long rain,
At last the day prescribed for rural scampers!
We purchased bread and pates and a bottle of Champagne
And loaded up our wicker picnic hamper.

We packed some chilled smoked salmon and some Winnipeg cream cheese,
Our cake was angel food, our eggs were devilled,
We took a home-made afghan we could spread beneath the trees,
Our plates were marked Limoges, our wine flutes bevelled.

Encumbered thus with butter, booze, and ripe and runny brie,
And other foodstuffs loathed by lithe Jane Fonda,
We lifted up our hatchback, clicked our heels and said, "We're free!"
And hit the highway in our ageing Honda.

The trusty car devoured the miles, we fled the urban blight.
The open sky was blue, by clouds unruffled,
The sun sent us a telegram of warmth and golden light,
We read it while we snacked on chocolate truffles.

We crested one small rolling hill and saw a fragrant field,
Where flowers flounced to tempt the swooping swallows.
"Just like a painting by Cezanne!" you trilled. The car brakes squealed:
We hopped a fence and found a verdant hollow.

You spread our woolly afghan out, I cracked the Chardonnay,
You disabused the hamper of its dishes,
We spread our feast before us, raised a glass up to the day
And praised whatever gods had heard our wishes.

The picnic we devoured fast—the food scarce grazed our forks,
The Chardonnay we likewise quickly guzzled.
The cool Champagne was warming, so we freed it of its cork:
One glass, then two, and we began to nuzzle.

If there are children present, I'd advise you send them out:
For just as sowing seeds must lead to threshing,
When wine-drenched grownups start to nuzzle there is little doubt
They're on the twisty path to full-scale meshing.

And sure enough we shed our clothes and meshed there in the grass,
The remnants of our feast lay all around us.
What cared we if the birds or bees should see us as they passed
Or if some hopping rabbit family found us?

In harmony with nature we two revelled in the sun,
And when we had no fuel left for stoking,
We fed each other bits of brie upon a crusty bun,
And rued the day that we both gave up smoking.

But all at once a shadow fell. We looked up to the sky.
We saw no clouds, but in a trice determined,
Our frolicsome encounter had been latterly espied
And gaped at by a gawking group of Germans.

Their tour bus was parked nearby. They'd paused to take some air,
And scout about for some terrain to hike on.
They stood about our picnic site with unrepentant stares,
Then, as a group, began to click their Nikons.

Was this revenge for wars they'd lost? We grabbed our duds and food,
Love's temperature now hovering at zero.
We fled our shredded Paradise and ruptured loving mood,
And muttered curses learned from *Hogan's Heroes*.

At first we fumed, but now we laugh each time that we recall
Our pell-mell rush in half-slung shirt and tunic.
Oh, how I wish that I could be a fly upon the wall
When someone shows their slides back home in Munich.

MÉNAGE À QUATRE

A woman wrote from Saskatoon to say simply that she carried her cat, Pickle and ferret, Sable around with her in a backpack. The Poet, inspired by Edward Lear, took her situation and invented this tale of a shipboard romance. This was written some years before Mr. Richardson began his association with Romana Clay, R.N. It demonstrates a early predilection for the medical profession.

The ferret and the pussycat went off to sea
In a beautiful burgundy purse:
—Or rather a backpack—as part of the baggage
Of Roger, an unhappy nurse.

Roger, the nurse, was besotted with love
For a pediatrician named Anne.
But Anne had said, "Roger, I've got my career,
There's no room in my life for a man."

Unlucky Roger wept copious tears
When Anne broke this heart-wrenching news.
He cashed in his pension and bought matching luggage
And went on a twenty-day cruise.

His wish was to stanch this unfortunate passion,
Forget his physician so fickle:
He took as companions his ferret and kitty
Who answered to Sable and Pickle.

Now Pickle and Sable were honest and loyal
As Anne had been callous and feckless.
Though no one could question their virtues or manners
To bring them along had been reckless.

For ships harbour sailors who pack superstitions
Along with their cargo and nets,
And nothing makes sailors more edgy and wary
Than heading to sea with a pet.

But Roger, the nurse, was a creature of science:
He found such old wives tales a drag.
He said, "I know Sable will stay in my backpack,
The cat won't get out of the bag."

Roger was right. His two pets kept their counsel
And no one had cause to suspect
That Roger was packing a cat and a ferret
While strolling about on the deck.

And no one suspected a ferret and kitty
Were kipping each night in his bunk.
Then one day the Captain—a woman called Julie—
Saw Roger and said, "What a hunk!"

The very same evening she gave him the honour
Of coming to dine at her table:
But just as the steward was tossing the salad
His pack twitched and Julie met Sable.

Then Pickles the cat made a sudden appearance.
Julie, the captain, went pallid.
Roger'd forgotten that Sable and Pickle
Were partial to good Caesar salad.

Julie was stunned by this startling display
Of quadrupeds, sleek and eclectic.
She leapt from the table and shrieked out the door
Looked harried—in fact, apoplectic.

The crew and the passengers ran to the deck
At the sound of their crazed captain's curse.
Roger strode right to the fore of the crowd:
"Stand back!" he exclaimed, "I'm a nurse!"

"He's a nurse, he's a nurse!" said the tremulous throng,
Who knew that he'd quickly improve her.
Everyone hoped that he'd have to resort
To electrodes or Heimlich manoeuvres.

But Roger had other ideas in mind.
Said he, "Though it may not seem couth,
Her state of mind dictates a perilous course,
And so I'll employ mouth to mouth!"

Roger grabbed Julie in primitive fashion:
She found the whole business disarming,
Reacting in much the same way that Snow White
Responded when bussed by Prince Charming.

Feminists know that this all goes to show
That Julie was sadly benighted.
But what can I tell you apart from the truth?
The fact is that she was delighted!

Captains can marry a couple at sea
And Julie seized on that prerogative.
She carried off Roger away to her cabin
And popped him the big interrogative.

"I will," answered Roger. "You'd better," said Julie,
And Roger soon proved that he would.
They neither dissembled, perhaps the earth trembled,
And everyone thought it was good.

The rest of the cruise they all whiled away
With love and music and laughter:
Pickle and Sable and Julie and Roger
En route to a grand everafter.

BUT FOR A CONSONANT

Another poem with a medical theme. A nurse, representing her hospital's social committee, wrote to the Poet to report that on St. Patrick's Day, the institution would be sponsoring something called Potato Madness. The concept, which struck the Poet as a a tad on the arcane side, was for staff and patients to decorate potatoes, and in this way build something like camaraderie. Well, it takes all kinds. The Bard cast his mind back to the Mr. Potato Head he loved as a child, and came up with this bit of oddness.

Once upon a graveyard shift five nurses in obstetrics—
Nancy, Randy, Chloe, Prue and Myrtle—
Were boning up on enemas and different diuretics,
To pass the time while waiting for the fertile.

Myrtle sighed and closed her book—a bulky work on sutures—
And said "I'm feeling listless, tired and bland!
Let's organize some kind of fete, not in the distant future,
But soon! Let's have champagne and hire a band!"

"St. Patrick's Day is coming up," said Chloe, born in Galway,
"Why don't we pay our homage to its symbol?
We'll honour the potato in our every room and hallway,
And decorate them with our fingers nimble!"

"Oh! *Quelle idée!*" exclaimed her friends in continental manner,
"The very thing to warm our sluggish blood!
Let's find some crepe and bunting and devise a cunning banner
That reads, 'Come out and decorate a spud!'"

The nurses clapped their hands with glee! Oh! What an inspiration!
It struck a rich and resonating chord:
Soon each nurse and orderly was planning some creation,
Potato madness lived on every ward.

The doctors caught the fever, too. The patients were a-flutter:
Each spoke of how his spud would take all prizes.
Where once they thought of spuds as best with chives and gobs of butter,
They saw them now bedecked in other guises.

It didn't matter where you went throughout the halls of healing,
Potatoes were the stuff of each oration.
And if you asked a patient to disclose how she was feeling,
She'd only talk of spuds and decoration.

Then finally the great day dawned: The feast day of St. Patrick!
The spuds were trotted out in all their glory!
Some brought one, and some brought two, some hoped to score a hat trick
By entering in several categories.

There were spuds dressed in sombreros, there were tubers dressed in tuxes,
There were sweet potatoes waiting to be rated;
The atmosphere was friendly, there were teasings and "Ah shuckses!"
And spud on spud all preened and decorated.

The judges were assembled for their studied contemplation:
Each one was an honest, stern inspector.
They hardly had commenced their long, profound deliberation
When up the stairs there came a startling spectre.

Each judge turned and each judge froze where he or she was standing:
Their jaws were hanging level with their chests.
For there before them, all stark naked, standing on the landing
Was what they recognized as Dr. Best.

Kindly Dr. Best! He was a much sought out physician!
A specialist in tummy tucks, and lifts,
It didn't seem quite right for one in Dr. Best's position
To show his colleagues all his private gifts.

He was absolutely starkers, save for one small decoration:
A yellow ribbon knotted in a bow.
Otherwise he only wore a look of expectation,
As well as what you'd call a festive glow.

He'd tied the yellow ribbon to a vantage point strategic,
He'd fastened it where everyone could see.
"Tie a yellow ribbon," whistled Rose, from orthopedics,
But this one wasn't hanging from a tree.

"Sorry to be late," trilled Dr. Best all flushed and festive.
"Am I the only one to doff my duds?"
Murmers filled the air. The natives all looked rather restive.
"Is this the place they pick the best dressed stud?"

"Spud!" cried everyone at once, "not stud, you hapless twit!"
Poor Dr. Best displayed a body blush.
His ribbon slipped and Rose from orthopedics had a fit,
And Dr. Best departed in a rush.

For several minutes panic reigned, then someone gave a chuckle.
Giggles soon gave way to wholesale laughter
Everyone guffawed until their knees began to buckle,
And mirth was ringing from the very rafters.

Eventually calm reigned again. The judges did their duty.
They gave out ribbons, ending the hysteria.
There's still one left for Dr. Best and he can claim his booty:
But first he has to come back from Nigeria.

THE OFFICE PROJECT

An archivist wrote to request a poem for a colleague who was going on maternity leave. The Poet had noted that babies who gestate in office situations become the property of the group. This is the observation that informs the poem.

She turned up in the morning looking green around the gills
Thus dredging up suspicion there was money in the till.
The night we went for dinner and she didn't touch the wine
We theorized she'd found that there were jewels in the mine.
The phone calls from the doctor and the plenitude of snacks
Led us to surmise that there were groceries in the sack.
The salads that she favoured and the cigarettes she'd shun
Drove us all to speculate the oven held a bun.
We didn't want to egg her on, we didn't want to pry
Or ask overtly if the rabbit lived or if it died,
We didn't want to nose around, we didn't want to pester
Or say we'd noticed anything throughout the first trimester.
We excised from our lexicons such words as "child" or "birth",
Averting our collective glance from her expanding girth.
Although we pondered endlessly the question: girl or boy?
We never broke our silence and allowed her to be coy.
We simply waited patiently till one day she revealed
The source of her spare tire was the hub of a new wheel.
"No!" we said, in mock surprise. Then came the escalation
From "My my my!" to "Goodness me!" to "Hey! Congratulations!"
And from that very moment, without need of a directive,
We coalesced and formed a kind of baby-watch collective.
"How ya feelin' honey?" we inquire when she comes in,
And look concerned if she seems pale, or tired or wan or thin.
"And how's our little Thumper, how's our wiggly little worm?"
We ask and giggle when she yelps each time the baby squirms.

We look to see she's eating right, evaluate her lunch,
And speculate upon the sex, articulate each hunch
About the baby's prospects for a life of wealth and fame,
And almost come to fisticuffs deciding on a name:
We floated Ann and Jason. They both promptly sank like lead.
We tried out all the simple names like Helen, Stan and Fred.
We looked up fancy monikers, and gave them all their chance:
But Brittany reminded us a bit too much of France,
And Chelsea smelled of London, while Ondine engendered wrath,
We couldn't think of Sylvia without appending Plath.
A state of nervous tension reigned. We felt like nervous wrecks.
And when she had the amnio and didn't ask the sex,
Which would have eased the tension some, we felt a little miffed:
But not so piqued we don't call out each time she bends to lift
A pencil or a paperclip or other hefty weight:
"Put that down! Remember that you're in a fragile state!"
Everyone is pitching in to aid this noble cause.
Tomorrow we're all signing up for lessons in Lamaze.
The work is hard but shortly we'll all have the big reward,
Yelling "Push!" and helping her physician snip the cord.
And oh, but we'll have endless fun throughout the coming years.
We're looking for a college and we're checking out careers.
Whether you have Betty-Ann or whether you have Bobby:
You'll have got a baby. As for us, we'll have a hobby.

GENERAL MALAISE

*This rather militaristic little poem is the Bard's all-purpose answer to those who think **their** cold is so special it deserves a poem of its own.*

My body was tranquil land, an island in the sun,
A sort of fleshy Club Med for the bones,
Where organs toiled day and night until their work was done
And each one kept a neat and tidy home.

The liver and the pancreas would labour in the fields,
The little baby bladder never howled,
The stomach opened up its home three times a day for meals,
And anyone could drop in on the bowel.

To this mannered Paradise came General Malaise
To engineer his swift and bloodless coup:
He strapped his rusty sabre on, and donned his tassled fez
And raised the flag of mild, mid-autumn flu.

He did not meet resistance when he mounted his invasion
No counteraction came from secret cells.
It was as if the populace within my corporal nation
Collectively caved in, and sighed, "Oh well!"

"I'll throb if you would like me to," the forehead volunteered,
And opened up the temples, like a traitor.
Thus General Malaise gained easy access to the ears,
The two of whom were swift collaborators.

They channelled all his messages, his whispers of subversion,
They telegraphed his vile communiqués,
And hastened thus his brand of sweet and genial coercion.
He won the battle in a single day.

No one bothered to resist. There was not one defender,
No one threw a spear or fired a gun.
The sinuses, I guess, will be the last ones to surrender:
And even they, it seems, are on the run.

So General Malaise set up his temporary beachhead:
It may just hold a day or maybe two.
But while he reigns I'm nothing but a vapid, rattling bleachhead.
My compliments, *mon Général.* ACHOO!

HYACINTH

Hyacinth is the nom de plume of a woman from a small town in Nova Scotia. The poem was requested by one of her friends who was pleased with the the way "Hyacinth" dealt with a manipulative bounder who had made a graceless exit and wanted to get back on board.

Then here's the tale of Hyacinth, a zaftig *demoiselle.*
She had a pealing giggle, and her shape was like a bell.
Her shape was like an hourglass, all full and round and ample,
Impressive flying buttresses bedecked her body's temple.
And Hyacinth was happy with her corporal architecture.
She scorned the cult of thinness, disregarded pious lectures
Delivered up by beanpoles who were positively phobic
About the press of flesh and were addicted to aerobics.
Hyacinth cared not to hear their simpering reports.
Life's too short, she'd say, to shun the lure of Sachertorte.

Hyacinth's affiliate—let's call the bounder Ted—
Dropped by several times a week expecting to be fed.
She'd ply the callow fellow with a plate of scrumptious rations,
Then clothes were shed and Ted was led to bed for feasts of passion.
This went on for several months, but then there came a shift.
Hyacinth perceived her friend's attention start to drift.
He still came by to taste her wares, and ate just like before,
But once the food was finished Ted would scurry for the door.
He didn't stop to linger once he'd filled his gaping mouth,
His compass, evidently, only pointed to the south.

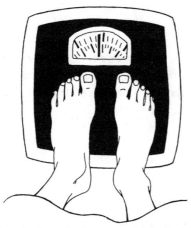

It wasn't long before she learned, through slightly devious means,
That Ted had found another who was dim and trim and lean.
Hyacinth was furious and she knew just what to do.
She called him and berated him and told him they were through.
She did it with bravado but her confidence was shaken.
She felt herself bereft, alone, forgotten and forsaken.
She looked at her reflection in the honest full-length mirror.
"Perhaps I am too fat," she sobbed and shed a glistening tear.
"I guess that's why he dumped me," and she made a sobbing sound,
Resolving then and there that she would shed some twenty pounds.

She'd said to Ted good riddance, but she secretly aspired
To win him back. With foolish hopes her furnaces were fired.
And so began her regimen of self-imposed starvation.
Hyacinth determined she'd effect her own deflation.
And oh, but she was miserable! She swore she'd gladly die
To have a small and sinful taste of chocolate pecan pie.
She tallied every calorie, embraced each crazy diet—
Nothing seemed too rad or mad. She'd simply buy and try it.
Oprah's magic liquid plan, or Liz's quick solution:
Six months passed and Hyacinth achieved her resolution.

With grim determination she achieved the poundage melt.
Hyacinth, once zaftig, was now positively svelte.
Ted got wind of what she'd done, and hurried round to look.
Oh boy, he thought, a girlfriend who is thin and who can cook.
He pleaded that she take him back. On bended knee he begged.
She took him in and filled him up with treats from Jenny Craig.
Hyacinth watched Teddy eat. She noticed that he slurped.
She saw his dirty collar and the grease spots on his shirt.
She noticed he had dandruff, and with several chins was blessed.
Ted, it finally dawned on her, was slovenly, a mess.

Was it for this she starved herself? She looked at him again,
And knew that, temporarily, she must have been insane.
When Ted had wolfed the supper down, he whispered, "Let's retire,
And take up where we left it off, rekindling the fire.
Let's do it babe, I'm dynamite! There's no time left to lose!"
"As I recall," said Hyacinth, "you've got a two inch fuse.
Take a hike you low life jerk! You're rude and crude and crass."
She threw him out and ordered up a pint of Häagen Dasz.
Hyacinth is free at last of Ted and all his tedium,
And in her dietetic life, she's found a happy medium.
She's taken all her diet books and put them on a shelf.
Now she's neither fat nor thin. She's happy with herself.

THE MIDDLE YEARS

A depressing little ditty, written at the request of a Toronto woman whose husband was obsessed with the signs of ageing. The reader might discern that the Poet's heart is well and truly in this one. The reader would be right.

Your middle years have come to call. They make a brutish din.
They travel not on kitten's paws—the crow's feet bring them in,
Your scotch is now a double. So's your bypass. So's your chin.
You're suddenly expected to be sage.
You notice that you're growing stooped. Your breath is indiscreet.
You ride the bus and thoughtful teens inquire, "Need a seat?"
You still do your aerobics, but each session leaves you beat:
Congratulations! This is middle age.

The hair that once bedecked your skull now bristles in your ears,
Your face shows new geography each time you pass the mirror,
You once bought Cosmopolitan, but now you browse through Lears,
You know that you have turned that certain page.
When sex is over far too fast, and sleep is done too soon,
And lunch is all you're after when you go back home at noon,
And condoms that you bought last year prove useful as balloons:
Then this is well and truly middle age.

When dogs and tiny children are a wee bit of a trial,
And liberal notions once embraced engender fits of bile,
And mounds of earth don't come to mind when someone mentions "pile",
You know that you have reached that special stage!
When midnight comes and finds that you are seldom still awake,
And getting up means opening a catalogue of aches,
You're rich enough to have but far too fat to eat the cake:
Then rest assured that this is middle age.

Your spousal unit yawns when you admit to an affair,
You hear yourself inform the kids their music's din and blare,
You still regret the dreadful day that Sonny split with Cher,
The fuel that keeps you going on is rage,
You look at your reflection and you whisper "Get a life",
And so you change your therapist, your husband, lover, wife,
And all the while you feel the deeper twisting of the knife:
Oh boy, oh boy! That sounds like middle age.

When suddenly your waistline measures bigger than your chest,
You visit the optometrist and fail the bloody test,
And after supper you lie down for "just a little rest",
Then there's no doubt you're trapped in midlife's cage:
You're caught behind the bars and there's no way of getting out,
It does no good to whine your plaintive existential doubts,
Remember when you rant and roar and kick and scream and pout—
That all things end—including middle age.

UNCLE TOVE

The principal challenge here was to find something to rhyme with Tove. The Poet feels confident that he succeeded. This poem, and the next, are portraits of those who age gracefully and happily. This he wishes for everyone.

My dear old uncle came to stay, my Swedish uncle, Tove;
He's hale and thrives at 95, and only eats anchovies.
He says that's why he's fit and spry and bright of eye and thin.
He owes it to anchovies that he eats straight from the tin.
He sucks each salty fillet down with Scandinavian lust.
He'll only eat a pizza if you hold the cheese and crust.
He only wants anchovies, unadorned by crust or toast:
This kind of guest's by far the best if one is playing host:
No need to shop for groceries, or explore some new cuisine,
No need to book a table in a place he's never been,
He never dirties cup or plate or spoon or fork or knife,
He just turns down the tinny top and gets on with his life.
And I am sure that he'll endure and not shake hands with death.
The reaper will keep walking when he scents old Tove's breath.
But that is neither here nor there. This poem, for what it's worth,
Is meant to say that Tove is a steward of the earth.
Reduce, Re-use, Recycle is his passion and his motto:
He likes to hike and often bikes. He's never owned an auto.
He's silver-haired but in his heart he's green as green can be:
This year when he came to stay he brought a living tree:
A handsome, bushy conifer, contained within a tub,
Eight feet tall and full and round, no puny little stub.
"I brought you this to decorate," he fishily exhaled.
But when I got the tinsel out, he ranted and he railed:
"No, no, no, not stuff like that! You use it by the handful,
Then throw it out so it can clog some overburdened landfill.
Start by thinking green! I mean the two of us can cobble
Something harmless to the earth, a clever homespun bauble!

Let's take these old anchovy tins. Ah yes! The very thing!
Think how grand they'll look when we have hung them up with string!"
So that's exactly what we did, and cleaving to his wish
Festooned the tree with tiny tins that once were home to fish.
And oh but it was glorious! The tree, the tins, the light!
Reluctantly we went to bed, and left the pretty sight.
I fell asleep and when I woke, the clock read 4 AM.
I thought that from the living room I heard a kind of hymn,
I thought I heard a song of praise, a chant so fine and rare.
Tove had awakened too. We tiptoed down the stairs.
It never once occurred to us we might surprise a thief,
Whoever made so sweet a sound could never bring us grief.
Whoever made so sweet a sound was gentle and inspired.
We snuck into the living room, and there beheld the choir.
Every cat from all around had come on silent feet,
And slipped in through the window—they were ever so discreet,
Attracted by the odor of the baubles that we'd strung
They sang their kitty carols where the scented tins were hung
Tabbies, Persians, Siamese, and half a dozen Manx
Stood about our Christmas tree and sang their song of thanks.
Around the heady tree they danced, not knowing they were seen:
They tapped the tins that made a sound like mini tambourines.
All agape we stood and stared. For half an hour we watched them.
How glad I am we hung the tins, and didn't think to wash them.
We finally tiptoed back to bed, just me and uncle Tove.
"Gloria Deo," sang the cats, "Thank God he made anchovies."

UPSTAIRS, THEY GATHER ROSEBUDS

This transpired in Winnipeg. The Poet would like to say that he is perfectly aware that the novella mentioned in Stanza nine is "The Turn of the Screw." Accuracy must sometimes be sacrificed for the sake of scansion. Mr. James would understand.

I'm in my early 70s. The world is now my oyster.
I'm taking everything it has to give.
My mother, when she reached my age, was virtually cloistered
While I have only just begun to live.

I bristle at the thought that age has made me narrow-minded,
Or that I've grown parochial in my views,
Or that I've put on blinkers that have left me nearly blinded
To everything that's trendy, bright, and new.

I read the latest novels, go to theatre and movies,
From time to time I like to go on dates.
I'm not what you'd call celibate. In fact, I think it's groovy
To feel the welling, primal urge to mate.

I'm of a generation, though, that values sweet discretion:
Discretion, which is valour's better part.
I do not kiss and tell. When I've enjoyed an amorous session
I do not dress my sleeve up with my heart.

I've learned these things with age. I know that youth, too, has its reasons:
I know that when the hormones start to surge
That summer, winter, spring or fall can be the mating season
And lustiness requires an urgent purge.

B. Horne

I know that the ensuing flail and mesh of limb and fluid
Is normally a reason to rejoice.
And youngsters, most especially, are certain when they do it
To demonstrate their pleasure with the voice.

I know my upstairs neighbours to this rule are fast adhering
For each and every time that they make love
I'm obliged to fill the role of she who's overhearing
The moaning and the thrashing from above.

I feel like a cartographer. I know their passion's atlas,
And read their recreation like a map.
First the cloying giggles, then the squeak of spring and mattress
Then the well-worn route of tiny gasps.

They're certainly enthusiasts. They certainly adore it.
I hear each sweet endearment that they coo.
I sigh and pick a book up and endeavour to ignore it.
Last night I read "The Turning of the Screw."

And when I'd finished Henry James, and still they hadn't finished,
I turned my mind to charitable thoughts,
Hoping that my sense of angst would somehow be diminished
If I begrudged them not their happy lot.

How wonderful they're fit and so adept at their gymnastics!
How grand that loving makes them want to sing!
How thrilling that they're flexible, sufficiently elastic
To leap up to the chandelier, and swing.

But ah, my dear! It did no good. The only sound solution
Was waiting for their energies to flag.
While lying there and basking in their lusty noise pollution
I contemplated buying them twin gags.

Perhaps I'll just buy earplugs though, for youth must have its pleasures.
They're young, and soon enough they'll study care.
And when they've reached an age when they require gentler leisures
I hope some lusty couple lives upstairs.

ENVOI

Go softly, Gentle Reader:
You've exhausted now the trove.
The Poet wishes all of you
A life replete with love.

I also have advice for you,
My pearly words are these:
Rest well. Take an aspirin.
Put your head between your knees.

R.C., R.N.

THE CRAFT

OF

CORPORATE

JOURNALISM

WRITING AND EDITING CREATIVE

ORGANIZATIONAL PUBLICATIONS

LIONEL L. FISHER

Cover: Collage by Ruth Spani-Phinney, beachrasp@yahoo.com.
Cover design by www.HTMPublishing.net.

Library of Congress
Cataloging-in-Publication Data
Fisher, Lionel L.
The Craft of Corporate Journalism:
Writing and Editing Creative Organizational Publications /
Lionel L. Fisher
1. Business writing, editing. 2. Journalism, Commercial. 3. Journalism, Corporate, Consumer. 4. Employees' magazines, newsletters, brochures, etc. 5. Authorship. 6. Corporations 7. Publishing. I. Title.

www.lionelfisher.com

For Jane, Madeline, Mike, and Andy, who share the love of writing.

CONTENTS

The Organizational Communicator: Who, What, Why

The corporate journalist: A professional profile. Who you are. What you do. For whom you do it. Your growing importance in every public and private sector. The state of your craft. Why service journalism is such a fertile field.

Learning the Craft: A Solid Grounding

Expunging bafflegab. Striving for simplicity. Muting passive voice. Staying active with action verbs. Getting back to basics: Usage, grammar, punctuation, style. Questioning voraciously, checking endlessly. Passion firing excellence

Style: The Personality of Your Writing

Slipping the tethers, breaking the rules, going your own way. Humanizing copy, enjoying the language. Being yourself, letting it show. Succeeding, failing with enthusiasm. The organization writer's greatest fear. One reader at a time

Off with a Bang: Building Powerful Leads

The most crucial words: Your first. Why it's called seduction. A single criterion: Whatever works. Types of leads: Weather reports to eloquence. Building a repertoire of openers. Borrowing from fiction. Humor in corporate publications

The Feature Story: Grab Hold, Hang On
Elements, structure, organization, pace, flow. Backing in. Nut grafs. Stitching your story with an angle. Imagery through details. Showing more than telling. Importance of lists. Connectives. Culling quotes. Closing loops. Graceful exits

The News Story: Still an Inverted Pyramid
News story structure, organization, elements: Still five Ws and an H. Summary and secondary leads. How reporting has evolved, altered, stayed the same. Growing similarities in news and feature stories. Gaining momentum

The Vital Art of Interviewing
Setting the tone of interviews, assuring their quality. Maximizing precious time. Knowing what you're after, ways to get it. Doing your homework. Breaking the ice, parking your ego, building rapport, listening empty. Debriefing yourself

Writer's Block, Jump-Starts, Creativity
Dissolving writer's block. Lowering your standards temporarily. Quitting in the middle on purpose, jump-starts, incentives, necessary retreats. Ways to nurture, kill creativity. Resisting regimentation, encouraging "abnormalcy."

Defining, Tailoring Your Publication
Contouring the publication. Formalizing editorial objectives. Getting to know your readers. How, when to push their buttons. Earning credibility. Readership surveys. Understanding what you're after, how to get it. Editorial committees

Setting Your Publication's Style

Defining your publication's style. Establishing editorial rules, uniformity, guidelines. Choosing, adhering to one style guide or drafting your own. On not being awed by "experts." The importance of stylistic consistency

Soup to Nuts: Serving All Palates

Main courses to condiments, hors d'oeuvres to pastries, soup to nuts: A menu for every palate. Nutritious food for thought. Publication contents: News stories, features, columns, sidebars, pull quotes, headlines, captions, kickers

Involving Your Readers, Working with Others

The value of entertainment. Involving readers with human interest features, employee/customer/department profiles, slogan/photo/essay contests. Swipe files, recycling story ideas. Sharing the limelight

Everything I Know and Don't Understand

Wish lists. What I've learned from a lifetime of writing. Things you should know, what doesn't matter. Counsel, commiseration on 10-percenters, cutting cards, sexist language, blue-collar prose, Goodbosses and the other kind.

INTRODUCTION

"When in doubt," counseled Raymond Chandler, "have two guys come through the door with guns." Potent advice for authors of potboilers, but corporate and organizational communicators need a bit more firepower. Because yours is writing beyond the realm of entertainment. It is writing that fosters action.

Transcending the mere delivery of information, it is the business of getting readers to *do* something as a result of reading your words. Such as buying a product or idea or ideal, behaving more responsibly, adopting a better attitude, voting more knowledgeably, or working harder, smarter, safer. Instruction, advocacy, motivation, and empowerment as well as information and entertainment are part of your job description.

Yours is journalism with a definite slant, specific points of view, ulterior motives, particular objectives, all tilted toward the company, institution, association, or agency employing you.

You are, most decidedly, an editorial lance for hire.

So it behooves you to know your organization, its mission, and audiences intimately. Your writing must be personable, engaging, human, and persuasive, even eloquent when the occasion demands. For though you have the closest thing to a captive audience any writer could hope for, there's no such thing in these harried times.

Little is read these days unless it's captivating enough to snare that most precious of modern commodities, our elusive attention, which must be earned with good writing.

Mostly, therefore, this book is about becoming a good writer. Or a better one. Unfortunately, few shortcuts lead to that goal, a lifelong quest, fired by the passion to achieve it.

This book, then, is about the love of putting words on paper, the thrill of doing it well enough to move your audiences to action.

It is about giving yourself more license than restraint, more possibilities than certainties, more freedom than conformity, for with too many rules comes rigidity.

Better to operate on the principle that there are as many ways to learn things as there are people to learn them.

And when it comes to learning how to write, imagination is more important than information.

I wish I could make things easier for you by giving you more information than inspiration in the form of other people's creativity. More solutions than motivation. More absolutes than possibilities. More answers than questions. More endings than beginnings.

But that is not the way to become a good writer. For the answers, the certainties, the solutions, when they come, must be yours, not someone else's.

CHAPTER 1

THE ORGANIZATIONAL COMMUNICATOR: WHO, WHAT, WHY

Service journalists. That's how an editor-in-chief described us to a roomful of corporate communicators. We are, he said, purveyors of ideas, of information, and inspiration through writing intended to produce a positive response.

Call what we do, then, action journalism. Transcending the mere delivery of information, it is writing with the expectation that our readers will *act* as a result of reading our words.

And because of what we expect from them as a result of our efforts, a huge difference separates our kind of writing from the standard journalist's. They report and analyze. We report and advocate. They help sell newspapers and magazines. We help achieve organizational goals by influencing action.

We create and enhance employee, shareholder, and customer confidence, build faith in corporate leadership, pride in its products. We heighten employee morale, foster belief in our company's intrinsic worth and trust in its mission.

Lofty Goals, Low Priorities

These are admirable goals. Yet despite qualifying as the most economical and effective of communication tools, organizational publications traditionally have served as training grounds, corporate communications boot camps, or more "responsible" duties within the company, later on.

Organizational writing and editing jobs, for the most part, remain transient occupations. Journalism and communications graduates continue to fill the rapid-turnover positions, their fresh-faced ranks infiltrated by an occasional administrative assistant or executive secretary with adequate word skills.

Little wonder, then, that corporate publications, the "house organs" of old, continue to be frustrating enigmas. Deemed necessary by most managers, particularly in the vital areas of human resources and employee relations, the obligatory periodicals persist, not so much as proven means of fostering company spirit and performance as from some vaguely perceived necessity.

Organizational publications, therefore, particularly those produced for employees (the core audience of most U .S. communicators), tend to be the most vulnerable in economic hard times — and the earliest casualties when operating budgets get strained.

Part of the problem stems from the difficulty in measuring an organizational publication's true effect on employee productivity, motivation, and morale. Or its stimulative effect on sales, on corporate imagery, and the positive influence wrought on stockholders and the financial community.

Formidable Obstacles

On the other hand, the dollars-and-cents impact of marketing, advertising, direct mail, and other promotional efforts is easily quantified and readily reflected in profit-and-loss statements. So these budgets are keenly assessed and constantly evaluated.

As a result, advertising agencies come and go. Marketing strategies are adopted, revamped, or abandoned. Originality is coveted, professionals hired, fired, excoriated, or exalted, not necessarily in that order. In short, attention is paid, success rewarded, mediocrity assailed, and excellence pursued.

Alas, not so in corporate communications.

But is all of this much to-do about nothing? After all, what real damage can ineffectual newsletters do? And when they're good, what real benefits accrue to their organizations? Plenty, claim the nation's organizational communicators.

4

When the ubiquitous, ambidextrous, multitasking newsletter and its organizational cousins, corporate magazines and newspapers, became popular in the 1950's, management, nonetheless, continued to view them largely as frills.

Predictably, therefore, hard times shrank communications budget first, and corporate editors were considered barely more than clerks. Nonetheless, many of them have moved to the core of management, stepping from their stack of publications into higher echelons of their institutions. And brought their organizational newsletters and magazines with them.

Today, organizations rely on their printed and on-line periodicals to communicate with internal and outside audiences. Most companies, institutions, associations, and government agencies publish at least one newsletter or magazine. Many produce several. Some in specialized fields turn out dozens. There's a good reason why.

Good communication goes straight to the bottom line. This phrase comes from the business world but applies to organizations of every kind. Instead of "bottom line" read "vision of success."

It isn't hard to figure out that people work harder, smarter, and happier when they're given regular, timely, honest, interesting news and information about their organization's goals in business and society — and their own roles in achieving those vital ends.

Be they managers, employees, customers, consumers, constituents, or opinion leaders, people who feel trusted and valued tend to respond with optimism, energy, and purpose.

The cost of a newsletter is probably the most worthwhile expenditure any [union] local can make," said Canadian Association of Labour Media President Katie FitzRandolph at a communicators' workshop.

"A newsletter," she remarked, "shows the members that the local leadership cares about them and respects their opinions, that it wants the members to be informed and aware of their rights, their resources, and what their union is doing for them."

Convenient, Authoritative

What's more, messages come in handy packages readers can examine when and where they wish. Amid the array of media available to most organizations, print and Internet communications are the most economical to prepare and the easiest to disseminate.

Newsletters are the medium of choice even when budgets aren't a controlling factor. When New York City's Transit Authority, for instance, decided to tackle the huge marketing problem of its subways, it published one of the most stylish newsletters ever devised by a city agency.

One reason management so favors the written word is because it is formal. It carries authority. Putting vital, complex messages in written form not only demands thoughtful preparation, it implies tacit support of the messages conveyed, which is why people respect organizational publications.

Still, respect is increasingly harder to come by because the credibility gap continues to widen: between industry and its publics, between manufacturer and consumer, management and labor, employer and employees, business and the news media.

Is there, then, a more accurate, effective, timely, cost-considerate tool to bridge these credibility canyons than organizational publications presented on-line or in print? But only to the extent that they earn the attention and credence of their readers. And readers bestow that credence only when the publication appears honest, factual, authoritative, and well-written. They ignore the others.

The popularity of corporate magazines and newsletters has resulted in their proliferation, though many of them go unread because they fail to grab and sustain the intended reader's interest. And that's your job.

Here is an arena in which to shine, where excellence glistens amid the drabness of unacceptable efforts. For most organizational publications are barely passable endeavors:

bland and predictable, downright boring. Can't sleep? Keep a few issues on your night table. They'll put you out every time.

Conversely, a stack of outstanding organizational publications can be a solid stepping-stone to success for their editor, the passport to a life after writing — or a life of writing, if that is preferred.

Whether you choose to remain a service journalist or try your hand at other corporate affairs, the ability to express yourself with precision and style will keep you in strong demand throughout your career. For the emotionally and financially rewarding opportunities for men and women grounded in corporate and organizational communications will continue to grow exponentially.

CHAPTER 2

LEARNING THE CRAFT:
A SOLID GROUNDING

If you're immediately at ease with a creative idea cautions an advertising adage, take another look. It's probably not an idea at all. We're comfortable with what's familiar, you see. What scares us is the new, the untried, the untested. So we stay with what's easy.

The danger for newsletter writers who grind out their copy issue after issue for a taken-for-granted audience lies in letting it all get too easy, settling for the knee-jerk response, the current buzzword, the all-too-familiar phrase, the comfortable approach, instead of always reaching for something more, something better, something original.

When adcrafters and organizational writers quit trying to peddle their products with originality and verve, lapsing first into complacent grooves and then languid ruts, their work settles into a quagmire of stale words and pale images.

Call it jargon, corporatese, bureaucratese, journalese, bafflegab, gobbledygook, doublespeak, or whatever else critics label bloated, desultory writing these days.

Whatever its name, it is a disease diagnosed by its symptoms: passive voice, strangled syntax, corpulent words, circuitous sentences, and tiresome verbosity.

Like chicks imitating a rooster's cock-a-doodle-do, we salt and pepper our presentations with our elders' lingo. We mistake big words for strong words, forgetting that the writing in the publications we admire is usually simple writing.

And therein lies the organizational writer's greatest pitfall: Trying to sound vague and pompous for the worst of reasons — because we think we should — until doing so becomes natural. And chronic.

Then one sad day we find we're incapable of turning out anything but this kind of ponderous writing, produced without much thought or effort. And we're in serious trouble.

Simply being aware of the easy allure of corporatese and bafflegab is the biggest step we can take toward sentences with snap, crackle, and pop — and away from those that run limply and interminably on like strands of buttered linguine dribbling off an overflowing plate. Plain talk is not easily achieved in corporate America, advises everyone's favorite writing guru, William Zinsser, for one reason: "Too much vanity is on line. Executives at every level are prisoners of the notion that a simple style reflects a simple mind."

Simple Isn't Simpleminded

The opposite, of course, is true. What's unclear in your mind will be unclear on paper. Hard work and lucid thinking produce precise words and potent images. Vague writing results from fuzzy reasoning. Or sheer laziness.

Something else results from mental laxity: the perilous cliché, every writer's insidious enemy, described by Eric Partridge, compiler of *A Dictionary of Clichés,* as "an outworn commonplace, a phrase or short sentence that has become so hackneyed that careful speakers and scrupulous writers shrink from it because they feel that its use is an insult to the intelligence of their audience or public."

Clichés are idioms beaten senseless, pummeled by repeated usage into stereotypes of expression so beyond redemption that they are an affront to the intelligence of readers.

Make no bones about it, not for love or money, at high noon, or in the dead of night, by the cold light of reason, in the final analysis, the spur of the moment, or twinkling of an eye, should you ever touch a cliché with a ten-foot pole, red-hot poker, sturdy oak, or whatever else strikes your fancy — catch my drift?

What kernel of wisdom, then, or nugget of advice to impart to the budding newsletter writer whose pursuit of excellence will be a lifelong quest at the very least? The best advice around is the time-honored KISS principle: Keep It Simple, Sweetheart.

Simplify, Simplify

In his classic primer, *On Writing Well*, Zinsser is passionate on the subject of writing simply. Strip every sentence to its cleanest components he exhorts: "Every word that serves no function, every long word that could be a short word, every adverb which carries the same meaning that is already in the verb, every passive construction that leaves the reader unsure of who is doing what — these are the thousand and one adulterants that weaken the strength of a sentence."

Ask yourself endlessly if every word is doing new and useful work, Zinsser urges. "Can any thought be expressed with more economy? Is anything pompous or pretentious or faddish? Are you hanging on to something useless just because you think it's beautiful?"

"Simplify, simplify," he concludes.

But why is this so hard to do? It's because organizations speak in proprietary tongues, because it's become too easy, natural, and effortless to lapse into the specialized verbiage we use daily, to which we've grown so accustomed.

There are words and phrases that have become an integral part of every industry and profession. For reasons of legal clarity and technical precision, organizational writers should not circumvent or alter this specialized mode of expression. But keeping legalese and jargon to a minimum is mandatory or it will suffocate your copy.

Writing in jargon may sound plain and familiar to those who speak the language, but it will be unintelligible to everyone else.

That's why technical writers get paid the big bucks — to translate the gobbledygook into intelligible, interesting, perhaps even entertaining prose.

Active Verbs Pace Copy

To accomplish this lofty end, first of all, we should banish the passive voice from our stylistic repertoire. Avoid it as you would poison oak on the path of your professional progress. Doing so may not always be possible, as in instances when you don't know the active subject or you can't easily state the subject. ("The building was vandalized.")

Or if the subject is evident from the context of the sentence. Or special circumstances — the need for tact, delicacy, deliberate obscurity, and so on — prevent you from identifying the active subject. ("Irene Blake was turned down when she first applied for work at…")

Or if you want to connect thoughts. ("The day was perfect, the food good, and the company friendly as some 350 Paper Group employees got together for a great outing on September 14.")

As a rule, though, try to use active verbs, not only to invigorate your sentences but to tighten them up as well:

Passive Voice: "The first blow was struck by him." "The floor was littered with trash." "The horse thief was hanged by the posse.

Active Voice: "He hit first." "Trash littered the floor." "The posse hanged the horse thief."

The difference between passive and active verbs is the gulf between pallor and passion. Chronic use of passive verbs assures what the word connotes — passivity — while active verbs blast your readers down the page.

Bureaucrats, academicians, politicians, and corporate executives thrive on the passive voice because it lets people off the hook, skirts blame, points limply at amorphous companies, institutions, agencies, divisions, and departments instead of singling out culpable individuals.

Passive voice turns straightforward verbs into obfuscatory nouns, clarity into uncertainly. "Deny" becomes "denial."

"Accuse" becomes "accusation." "State" becomes "statement." "Seize" becomes "seizure."

Passive voice obscures, obfuscates, stifles. It is tame, tepid, cautious.

Active voice clarifies, energizes. It is bold, vigorous, direct.

Exceptions to Every Rule

There are exceptions to this good rule, of course, as there are exceptions to every rule. Tom Paine's immortal line, "These are the times that try men's souls," would not have been improved by his substitution of an active verb: "These times try men's souls." The leaner verb forms a shorter sentence, true, but one that is lyrically diminished.

So what's right most of the time isn't right all of the time. That's what makes horse races and good writing. Use passive voice when you can't get around *not* using it, but check first to see if you can substitute brawnier words to form leaner sentences to project your thoughts with more vigor and verve.

Note how tepid verbs, weak construction, and passive voice slog through this glob of text from a state Department of Revenue communiqué: "Declarations of worthwhile purpose and charitable endeavors must be manifested in concrete endeavors and tangible reality which benefits the recipient. Unless this element of a gift or giving is present promises of future worthy endeavors are meaningless by inaction, and give the applicant no preferred status."

See how passive voice cripples this lead from a newsletter story on chemical additives: "One of the toughest challenges in formulating a lubricant is adequately controlling the rate at which oxidation reactions occur at elevated temperatures. Although modern base oils possess an oxidative stability that may be sufficient under normal demands, it is not sufficient for machinery running under high loads (compressors, gas turbines, and gears) or for those operating with large oil chargers (transformers, steam turbines and ship gears)."

Consider these lead graphs from a bank newsletter for customers:

> To successfully and actively participate in a rapidly moving highly technical, computerized society, some form of advanced education has become absolutely necessary. Without it an individual may be limited economically and socially.
>
> A college education is more important today than at any other time in our history. Because of rising education costs, declining financial aid and the effects of tax reform, paying for an education is not as simple as it used to be. Without proper planning it is almost impossible.

How much better this piece would have been had the editor simply deleted the first paragraph and led off with the second.

Short and Plain

Several years ago, International Association of Business Communicators' *Journal* carried an article titled "Reader Arousal: It Makes a Difference How You Write It." Yes, it does. Snappy headline, interesting topic, but here's how the author, a university communications professor, led off his piece:

> Arousal is a fundamental variable in human behavior and appears to have a particularly important mediating function in the mechanisms which guide human information exposure.
>
> In recent years, it has come to be used as a yardstick for assessing the likelihood that persons would turn away or continue to expose themselves to various kinds of communications stimuli.

Sounds more like a sex therapist than a communications professional. Whichever your profession, you'll communicate more clearly if you lose the jargon and psychobabble.

Organizational writing should energize, not enervate. Our mantras aren't meant to anesthetize. They should be a call to action, not ennui.

Yet, like warm rain on a tropical beach, passive voice in corporate prose saps the energy from our writing, lulling our readers into mindlessness, certainly not the effect desired by this annual report writer I'm sure:

> There was encouraging progress last year toward resolution of longstanding market uncertainties. A settlement of outstanding litigation was reached with a competitor, important federal and slate regulatory proceedings considering changes to the Alaska market structure moved closer to completion and aggressive marketing efforts began to have some effect.

Why not this instead?

> "We settled a major lawsuit last year, and sales spurred by improving market conditions have finally picked up."

More passive voice from a savings and loan report:

> There are many opportunities and challenges facing the financial services industry today. Increasing competition, continuing consolidation, and increasingly stringent capital regulations are but a few of the trends that will impact the industry's institutions.

> The approach to competing in such an environment is focused on long-term strategies aimed at maintaining profitability and increasing stockholder value. The company's ability to manage change and respond

quickly to opportunities and challenges will key its future success. This long-term management philosophy is one reason (the bank) has improved its financial strength and performance during a time of transition for the company and a period of turmoil in the industry.

Instead, how about this shorter, simpler paragraph?

It's tougher than ever to make a buck these days, so we didn't do too well last year. But things could have been a lot worse. Don't worry, though, we're hanging in there.

Intentional Ambiguity

Business people don't make their points so bluntly, of course, which is why passive voice is a deliberate choice. The justification of stultifying prose in annual reports and other corporate literature is that obfuscation is best achieved in financial reporting — not with supple, energetic writing that makes one simple point at a time, but with generic corporatese that wanders aimlessly through euphemistic thickets of grammatical underbrush.

And all that need be done to achieve the desired ambiguity is to allow the variegated, multi-departmental process of writing, editing, and endless approvals to waddle to its ponderous end.

As Kingman Brewster Jr. puts it, "If I take refuge in ambiguity, I assure you that it's quite conscious."

Another cynical view is that fuzzy writing is inevitable in organizational communications, akin to catching flu in the office once it starts going around.

Here's what a corporate professional wrote in a report to management: "In the area of formal written communications, the lowest dissemination-level vehicle has the highest credibility quotient." (Did he mean to say, "Of all the company publications, our mill newsletters are the most-trusted."?)

Inevitable Incomprehension

Thumb randomly through organizational publications and step back as incomprehensibility dribbles off the pages:

"In an environment characterized by constrained financial resources and intense competition..." ("In a tight, competitive economy...")

"Extension to private industry of a public law on rehabilitating the handicapped may become an effective means of expanding the tight U.S. work force." ("A law to help rehabilitate the handicapped may help U.S. employment.")

"Achievement of revenue growth..." ["More sales..."]

"...in a fraction of the time required previously." ["...quicker."]

"Beyond these generalities, differences in organizational characteristics and pay-analysis methods are associated with differences in relative job valuation. Finally, the absence of job gender and respondent sex effects suggests that pay differentials between men and women do not result from differential usage of job-worth information in pay-setting procedures, or from differences in the personal characteristics of individuals with pay-setting responsibilities." [I won't even try to translate that one!]

"...designed to contrast small firms with all the rest — to specify and to evaluate whether the differences between small firms and mid-to-large firms are matters of scale only, or instead, are differences in kind. While performance appraisal is the foundation for effective management of human resources, it is a difficult and complex process. Few things have an equal impact on the relationship between employee and supervisor or company than this annual rating of an individual's activities on the job." ["Few programs benefit employer-employee relationships as much as annual performance reviews."]

"It seems prudent, at the very minimum, to approach diversification by industry, geographic sector, risk ratings and collateral similarities. Provided this is done well, perhaps the risk of volatility will be mitigated. It is generally true that a diversified portfolio of risky assets is probably safer than a poorly diversified portfolio of somewhat less risky assets. But we must recognize the conventional concepts of diversification may fail to account for the potential impact of systematic changes (for example, recessions, interest-rate increases) on an LBO portfolio which otherwise may appear to be quite well diversified. [Note the expletives that lead off every sentence: "It seems prudent..." "Provided this is…" "It is generally true …" "But we must recognize…")

Bronx Cheers

Such writing rankles to the point of retaliation, says Gary Blake, head of a New York consulting firm offering language-skill courses. Blake lambasted the business world for its tedious writing with a series of "Percy" awards to underscore his contention that limpid corporate prose is "not only a linguistic liability but also a blow to productivity and profit."

In other words, anguage that fails to add, detracts.

To honor such ill-chosen language, the annual Percy (the name was coined from that most grating of corporate communication phrases, "Pursuant to your request") dubiously honors business letters and memos containing the most misused, ill-chosen, pretentious, absurd words and phrases currently in vogue. Categories include the "Mrs. Malaprop," the "Stuffed Shirt" (for entries distinguished by the most jargon-laden phraseology) and the "Run That By Me Again" (for the most convoluted submissions).

To prevent the nomination of your own copy for a Percy, put these ground rules to work immediately:

Short is usually better than long. Guard against using a long word when a short one will do. Or because the longer word sounds more important. Or because you're accustomed to using it. Or because it's the first word that comes to mind. Or for whatever reason that slows the reader and makes you appear pompous.

Question, for example, using "numerous" instead of "many." "Facilitated" instead of "made easy." "Individual" instead of "man," "woman," ";girl," or "boy." "Remainder" instead of "rest." "Sufficient" instead of "enough." "Attempt" instead of "try."

The cautionary examples are endless, but here are a few others commonly found in organizational publications and business correspondence:

This was used:	*Better:*
with respect to	about
effectuated	done, complete
at this point in time	now
in order that	so
attached herewith	here is
expeditious	fast
expertise	skill
magnitude	scope
state-of-the-art	latest
please feel free to	please, kindly
consequently	so
inception	start
was in consultation with	consulted
in the indefinite future	someday
in the near future	soon
at this point in time	now
in regard to	about
for the purpose of	to
accompanied	went with
has been couriered	was sent
has been messaged	was told
with great rapidity	quickly
substantial	much

selectively included	chose
whatever additional	any more
totally eliminated	got rid of
are in general agreement	agree
are a necessity	needed
prior to	before
held discussions	discussed
declined to comment	wouldn't say
accessed ore	mined
incarcerated	jailed
ingested	ate
gained entry	got in
architectural configuration	layout, design
heavily utilized	used often
thoroughly qualified	expert
methodology	way
disadvantaged, deprived,	have-nots
nonaffluent	poor
inner city	ghetto

The examples — and choices — are as myriad and plentiful as russet leaves in a Vermont October, but you get the idea.

Use adjectives and adverbs only if they contribute. Make sure they don't repeat the meaning contained in accompanying verbs and nouns, as here:

"The answer also includes..." ("Also" is superfluous in conjunction with "includes.")

"At this time we cannot foretell." ("At this time" is unnecessary because "foretell" means "to predict," thereby precluding present knowledge.)

"The answer has been drafted, served, and filed in this case." ("Drafted" can go; if the answer wasn't drafted, it couldn't be served or filed.)

"As soon as we received notice of the action, we promptly submitted copies." (Drop "as soon as" or "promptly" because they both mean the same thing.)

From a full-color ad in *The New York Times Magazine* for $2 million condos: "The most perfect penthouse in New York..." And from a Boca Raton Resort and Club newsletter: "It's hard to imagine a more perfect choice..." ("Perfect" means entirely without fault or defect." There are no degrees of perfection. The same goes for "complete" and "unique.")

From *Florida Golfer:* "...at Bay Hill, just a few short miles to the west of Isleworth." (Lose "short." Miles aren't long or short, they're exact distances. Also, the sentence would be crisper without "just" and "to the": "...at Bay Hill, a few miles west of Isleworth." Or "...at Bay Hill, just west of Isleworth.")

"Because of its close proximity." ("Close" is superfluous because proximity indicates nearness.)

"Annually, the company sells over fifty condominiums." ("A moon over Miami sounds appealing, but make it "more than fifty condominiums sold.")

"Start all over again." (Drop "all over" or "again.")

"Free gifts." (Gifts, by definition, are given freely.)

"Past experience" and "ancient history are good teachers." ("Past" and "ancient" are redundant: "Experience and history are good teachers.")

"A retired Army veteran..." (A veteran, by definition, is a former member of the armed services, thus retired.)

Use the possessive. Why use a prepositional phrase when a possessive noun would shorten the sentence and make it flow better? "The ruling of the board is pending." (The board's ruling...) "The work of the committee is almost completed." (The committee's work is almost done.)

Choose the precise verb. Don't take several words to convey a thought when a well-chosen one will do. Someone who's looking intently at you is staring. A driver who increases the speed of his car accelerates. Take the shorter route.

Make every word work hard. Would you miss the adjective or adverb if it wasn't there?" Cut every word that doesn't carry its own weight. And throw out qualifiers, words such as "kind of" and "sort of" and "somewhat" and "a bit." They're what E.B. White calls "the leeches that infest the pond of prose, sucking the blood out of words."

Don't hedge your opinions or soften your expressions with timidities. Be strong, lean, confident. Your readers will react accordingly.

Find the perfect word. Become a connoisseur of the language, always reaching for the exact word, ever wary of those that appear impeccably tailored to your thought but, in fact, are wrong, eroding precious credibility with readers who know better.

"Anxious," for example, implies apprehension and shouldn't stand in for "eager," which suggests enthusiastic anticipation. One is negative in tone, the other positive.

Too many writers consider the verbs "assume" and "presume" to be interchangeable. They're not. Both mean "to undertake" but "presume" has the added nuance of acting on presumption, without leave or clear justification.

Other writers freely substitute "podium" and "lectern," but they shouldn't. Podiums and daises are raised platforms positioned in halls or large rooms for speakers or orchestral conductors to stand *on* — not *at*. One stands at a lectern or reading desk, which is usually not wider than two or three feet. Have ticket agents, therefore, stand at a counter instead.

A grammatical error worth mentioning is the common phrase "between you and I." It is always between you and me.

Speaking of "between," how often that preposition appears when "among" is intended. Use "between" when two persons or things serve as the object. ("His choice lay between a rock and a hard place.") Use "among" when three or more options are considered collectively, or when no close relationship is intended, as in "a custom among Eskimos."

Compare "compare" and "contrast." To compare is to note similarities or differences in objects. To contrast is to emphasize differences only.

Nor are "convince" and "persuade" interchangeable. The former means to overcome by argument, while the latter suggests winning over by reason or inducement. What's more, a sentence such as "He convinced her to leave" is wrong, and the use of an infinitive following "convince" is an especially egregious error. "He convinced her she should leave" is correct, as is "He persuaded her to leave."

Consider, too, "occur" and "transcribe." "Flout" and "flaunt." "Fortunate" and "fortuitous." "Verbal" and "oral." "Historic" and "historical." "Present" and "current." Look 'em up! Similar doesn't mean identical.

Then there's "hat," mistakenly used in place of "which," and vice versa. Remember: *that* is the defining or restrictive pronoun ("The TV set that has to be repaired is in the closet."), while *which* is the non-defining or non-restricting pronoun ("The TV set, which has to be repaired, is in the garage.")

Another tip-off is that a comma always precedes *which* in the sentence, even though, as William Strunk suggests, *which* occasionally seems preferable to *that*. ("Let us now go even unto Bethlehem and see this thing, which is come to pass."). Always use the two pronouns consistently.

Also, don't have anyone feel *badly* unless you're trying to indicate an impaired sense of touch. People feel *bad* when they're emotionally down or physically ill. Verbs such as *feel, smell,* and *taste* are forms of the verb *to be* and often act as linking verbs. When they do, they merely state equivalences, so they take no objects, direct or indirect. You wouldn't say "His moves were suddenly." Or "The actors are badly." Neither, then, should they feel badly.

More examples of commonly misused words and expressions — 25 pages of them — are herded into a chapter in *The Elements of Style.* Authors Strunk and White noted these examples aren't so much manifestations of bad English as of bad style. "The commonplaces of careless writing," they called them.

Worth Checking Out

Getting uneasy? Less sure of yourself? Good! It's a healthy way for writers to be. "CHALLENGE AUTHORITY." That once-ubiquitous bumper sticker, should be hung on every organizational communicator's' word processor as well. Forever question the meaning, spelling, punctuation, and usage of each and every word you employ. Don't become smug about anything relating to your writing, clinging always to a steadfast rule: "If in doubt, check it out."

Whenever a word or phrase emits warning vibrations, reach instinctively for a dictionary (treat yourself to a new edition every year) or stylebook. Get in the habit of reaffirming current rules of grammar. Delight in looking up words. Understand the subtleties of meaning constantly offered, always asking if the nuances have altered through time or usage, and whether the shades of meaning are transposable in varying contexts.

Hordes of nouns, verbs, adverbs, and adjectives seem interchangeable but are different in meaning — either vastly or minutely different, but different nonetheless, therefore not ideal for every occasion.

Make every word fit every thought exactly. People don't just speak. They mutter, murmur, whisper, shriek, drawl, growl, chatter, bellow, and otherwise articulate their thoughts and feelings.

Look up the simple act of placing one foot after the other in your thesaurus. You'll find dozens of ways to do it. One can stroll, strut, shuffle, trudge, amble, shamble, or swagger, to mention just a few ways to ambulate. Why settle for just walking every time?

Become a dilettante, a connoisseur of the words you select. Be downright picky about every single one you employ toward your communications ends. "The difference between the right word and the almost right word," Mark Twain pointed out, "is the difference between lightning and a lightning bug."

Good writers are passionate — often crossing the line into paranoia — about the tools of their trade and how powerfully they can wield them. It's their passion about words that makes them prolific.

Punctuate properly. If you don't know how, as many college graduates don't, it's never too late to learn. Placing periods, commas, and apostrophes in their proper places, each and every time, is critical to your professional longevity. Get yourself a copy of William Strunk Jr. and E.B. White's pencil-thin *The Elements of Style.* You won't need another primer. Ground yourself, once and for all with their help, in correct grammar, spelling, usage, and style.

Are you certain, for instance, which punctuation marks belong within quotation marks and which don't? The *Associated Press Stylebook* advises that commas and periods should always be enclosed by quotes. Question marks and exclamation points, on the other hand, belong inside quotation marks only when they are part of the text being quoted. ("Who wrote the article, 'Brigadoon Revisited'?" "Have you read the article, 'Brigadoon Revisited'?" he asked.")

Etch into your brain the proper use of those pesky but indispensable periods, commas, dashes, apostrophes, colons, semicolons, quotation and question marks, parentheses, and ellipses. Nothing shatters the reader's trust in a writer as quickly as improper punctuation. The feeling is that if you haven't mastered something so basic to your craft as grammar and usage, how reliable is anything else you have to offer?

In UCLA screen writing professor Richard Walter's words, "If he can't get the easy stuff, how will he get the hard?"

There is nothing trivial about the mechanics of writing, Professor Walter stresses: "If writers don't nurture and protect language, who will?" he asks. "Typographical errors, rotten spelling, lousy punctuation, and sloppy grammar attest all too clearly to carelessness and imprecision — mortal enemies of good writing."

Look at it this way. How would you feel about an accountant who couldn't add?

CHAPTER 3

STYLE: THE PERSONALITY OF YOUR WRITING

Let's hear it for rules, guidelines, and principles. We all need them, especially in the beginning, because discipline is the foundation of excellence. "A few strong instincts, and a few plain rules" is how Wordsworth summed up the pursuit of excellence in whatever endeavor. And so it is for the creators of organizational publications.

But only to a point.

There comes — or should come — a time when you get good enough, confident enough, comfortable enough in your craft to depart from the norm, deviate from the familiar, slip the instructional tethers, ease your way into the white waters of more-flamboyant expression. Some call it *style*, this divergence from the paved, well-lit avenues of familiarity onto the less-trodden paths of innovation and creativity. And the better you become, the more restraints you can loosen, the clearer your personal style will show through the cautionary restrictions.

And shine through your words you should.

"Good writers," notes William Zinsser, "are always visible just behind their words. If you aren't allowed to use 'I' at least *think* 'I' while you write," he exhorts. "Or write the first draft in the first person and then take the 'I's out. It will warm up your impersonal style."

No Aesthetic Absolutes

Says American author John Gardner, "What the beginning writer ordinarily wants is a set of rules on what to do and what not to do in writing...some general principles can be set down...and some very general warnings...but on the whole the search for aesthetic absolutes is a misapplication of the writer's energy. When one begins to be persuaded that certain things must never be done...and certain other things must always be done, one has entered the first stage of aesthetic arthritis, the disease that ends up in pedantic rigidity and the atrophy of intuition."

"Try to cleanse your mind of what your English teachers told you," advises novelist-writing coach Rita May Brown. "They were reading with a different purpose from yours. They were also confining themselves to what has been generally accepted as high-quality *literature.* High quality, depending on where and when you went to school, can mean sterile and sanitized. Instead, think in terms of what works and what doesn't."

Brown's words ring as true for novelists and organizational communicators because grammatical impeccability is not the writer's primary goal. More important is getting what you write *read.* If that doesn't happen, then you've failed, regardless of the textbook correctness of your prose.

Going Your Own Way

So by all means cleave to the classic rules, starting with the one that says you don't break *any* rules until you've mastered them all. Novice wordsmiths could do worse than to pick up any of a dozen good style books and slavishly follow its dictates. But not until we've earned the right to diverge in the interest of stylistic vitality. Then it's a different story.

These opening paragraphs from a masterful word-portrait of Sammy Davis Jr., penned by Cynthia Gorney of *The Washington Post,* illustrate the point eloquently. Four of the first six paragraphs in Gorney's piece shatter a wise rule for beginning writers: achieve clarity, briskness, and pace with short sentences. She follows the rule in her terse opening paragraph:

He limps.

From two words, Gorney's second sentence leaps to 44:

He is losing his right hip — you might too if you had started dancing before the Great Depression and had danced ever since, danced and strutted and acted and joked and twirled and thrown your arms wide and belted your insides out in song.

Then to 59 words:

He danced when the movie directors told colored people to open their eyes real wide and sing about pork chops, and he danced when hotel owners would put a Negro on stage but refuse him a room for the night, and he danced when black men and women wore brilliant dashikis and glared at the pomade on his hair.

In her next paragraph, Gorney's first sentence returns to a recommended length, 15 words:

He danced in front of John F. Kennedy, and he danced in front of Queen Elizabeth.

But her next line soars again, this time to 51 words:

He danced on Broadway, and he danced on television, Don Rickles made fun of him, Frank Sinatra lifted shots of bourbon with him and magazines filled their pages with his marriage and his children and his rabbi and his jewelry and his great long cracked mashed nose, and still he danced.

The first sentence of Gorney's following paragraph drops to 38 words:

"Some people think Davis has a God complex," Dick Schaap wrote many years ago in the *New York Herald Tribune*, contemplating the exhausting matter of

29

Sammy Davis, Jr., "but this is absurd. On the seventh day, he works.

And her next paragraph contains only three words:

So he limps.

Four of the first seven sentences in the article total 192 words. And paring any of them would have detracted from the piece.

Think you could slip a 129-word sentence past your editor? Here's one by John Updike, from his *New Yorker* story, "Farrell's Caddie":

> At first, stepping forth on legs one of which had been broken in a college football game forty years before, and which damp weather or a night of twisted sleep still provoked to a reminiscent twinge, he missed the silky glide and swerve of the accustomed electric cart, its magic-carpet suspension above the whispering fairway; he missed the rattle of spare balls in the retaining shelf, and the round plastic holes to hold drinks, alcoholic or carbonated, and the friendly presence on the seat beside him of another gray-haired sportsman, another warty pickle blanching in the brine of time, exuding forbearance, and resigned, like Farrell, to a golfing mediocrity that would gradually make its way down the sloping dogleg of decrepitude to the level green of death.

A Time for Detours

Again, the point is to follow the rules, foremost among them those that guide you down the path of lean, supple language and a crisp, clean style. But on all literary roads you travel, you should eventually reach a juncture where the now-familiar signposts don't always impel you. Not if your prose is to soar.

Here's an example of generic ad copy. Many organizational writers still couldn't get away with a lead like the one below, despite the fact that sentence fragments typify modern advertising copy. Done well, these short-burst sentences move readers briskly through text they otherwise may have skipped:

> You cut the fat. Maybe some of the bone. You restructured. Shed businesses. Faced hostile takeovers, wrenching technological change and relentless global competition. Those were the good old days. Because tough as the 80's were, they were just a warm-up for the 90's.

Typically, someone in the corporate review gauntlet might attempt to "fix" the non-sentences by converting each shrapnel-like sentence into a proper declarative sentence with a subject and predicate verb. See how the text would have suffered in comparison — still not bad but not as incisive as the leaner, more-muscular ad copy:

> You cut the fat. Maybe you cut some of the bone. You restructured. You shed businesses and faced hostile takeovers, wrenching technological change and relentless global competition. Those were the good old days, because tough as the 80's were, they were just a warm-up for the 90's.

Correct May Not Be Right

This Nestle institutional ad typifies the shrapnel sentences favored by copywriters:

> How do you get to be one of the best-known companies in the U.S.?

> You think small. You do the little things well. So well, the big things take care of themselves.

Here at Nestle, that means growing perfect grapes for our Beringer, Chateau Souverain, Meridian, and Maison Deutsch wines. Choosing only the best noodles for our Stouffer Foods Macaroni and Cheese. Selecting only the choicest, most aromatic beans for our Nestle/Hills Bros. coffee blends.

Thinking small helps us run Nestles' U.S. companies. Make over 800 products. And maintain a century-old reputation for making only the very best. It also proves something we've always believed: Do all the little things right. And you'll wind up making a big name for yourself.

And some fast-paced prose from a Volkswagen marketing brochure. Note how the sentence fragments keep the pace briskly readable:

It's funny the things we remember. The things we hang on to. The first day of school. A first dance. A first kiss. Our first car. Some things are simply unforgettable.

One little thing can bring it all rushing back. A song on the radio. The smell of suntan lotion. Seeing an old friend at the beach. The friend you could always depend on

Everything was a little less complicated then. Tennis shoes didn't cost $200. A jukebox played your favorite song. And a car was part of the family. Right from the start.

What if quality never went out of style? What if originality still meant something original? What if simplicity, honesty and reliability came back again?

Imagine a new Volkswagen. A concept that redefines the automotive icon. Imagine a vision of high technology and advanced engineering. An expression of innovation, safety and performance. Imagine descendant of an enduring original. Different, unmistakable, yet true to its heritage in style and in spirit. Every line, every curve, every memory. Not just the evolution of a cherished classic, but the continuation of a worldwide love affair that began 21 million cars ago.

Innovation embodied in transition. A new Volkswagen concept. One look and it all comes back. But then, it never really left. The legend reborn. A friendship rekindled.

See how neatly the ad copy is tied together, front to back, cinched by a bright connecting bow, how the opening words instantly hook us, keep us reading through the marketing pitch, happy to stick around to the end because our attention has been earned and paid for.

Never Say Never

As for the time-honored rule of never ending a sentence with a preposition, never say never. Don't even say often. Forget, for example, which of the following sentences is "correct" and pick the one that best serves your readers: "This mess could take the rest of the day to get out of." Or "This mess could take the rest of the day out of which to get."

The "correct" sentence doesn't always make sense. So if ending a sentence with a preposition works, don't change it simply to conform to a musty rule. Especially if doing it goes against your writer's grain.

Let me rephrase that. If *correct* writing isn't *good* writing, then re-work the copy. What matters most is the effectiveness of your communications, not cleaving to old rules for their own sake. Being right is wrong if it stops readers in their tracks, period. If your words interrupt their journey through your prose, even momentarily, then they're the wrong words, regardless of how "correct" they may be.

"Sepulcher," for instance, is a verb as well as a noun, representing an action as well as a place. But what modern writer would sepulcher a dead body instead of placing it in a crypt?

"Even now," observes journalist Bill Bryson, "many good writers scrupulously avoid 'hopefully' and use the more cumbersome 'it is hoped' to satisfy an obscure point of grammar, which, I suspect, many of them could not elucidate...and there remains a large body of users who would, in Henry Fowler's words, sooner eat peas with a knife than split an infinitive."

"Those who sniff decay in every shift of sense or alteration of usage do the language no service," admonishes the English lexicographer Fowler. "Too often for such people the notion of good English has less to do with expressing ideas clearly than with making words conform to some arbitrary pattern."

The delight of our language is its never-ending volatility. It is a supple, ever-evolving organism that rewards our delight in its flexibility with energetic, joyful expression.

Anne H. Soukhanov, *Atlantic* magazine's "Word Watch" columnist, dramatized this constant kaleidoscopic change by trotting out a few words being tracked by editors of the *American Heritage Dictionary.* Noting that sustained usage will one day usher them into the dictionary, Soukhanov delights in a potential new verb: "exxon" — meaning to damage, especially by pollution — as in "Get this rust heap off the reef, mate, before you exxon the entire harbor." Or "I'm all thumbs — I tried to change the oil in my car and exxoned the whole driveway."

By the same token, the worst environmental disaster in history, which occurred on March 24, 1989 involving the Exxon Valdez in Alaska's Prince William Sound, may have retreated enough from our collective consciousness to warrant a more contemporary reference.

Again, it's strictly your choice. You're the writer.

Today's sports writers and commentators blithely turn nouns, adverbs, and adjectives into picturesque though nonexistent verbs as they laud athletes who "body hard," "vertical high," "chest" soccer balls, "audibilize" plays, "defense" their goals, and "outphysical" opponents.

During the 1992 Winter Olympics, "medal" became an ubiquitous verb as in "She's expected to medal in her event." "He medaled multiple times." "It's not whether you medal, but how hard you try." The best part of this trend is that it creates fast-paced thoughts by compressing several words into one to get readers where writers want them to go much quicker.

Even *The New York Times*

Even fastidious *New York Times* editors permit an occasional preposition-ending sentence such as one from reporter Suzanne Slesin. She chose to end the second sentence of her story's lead paragraph — after opting not to do so in her first sentence: "Forget about potted palms and intimate corners in which to rendezvous. There is no clock to meet under."

Not permissible under any circumstances, however, is the transgression of another rule which insists that participial phrases always refer to their grammatical subjects. Another *New York Times* reporter broke that rule by observing midway through a story, "After a long surveillance through Queens and Manhattan, the masked men drove the jeep back to the McCleans."

The resulting assumption is that the masked men did the surveilling, whereas the writer intended to convey it was the bad guys who'd been surveilled: "After a long surveillance of the masked men through Queens and Manhattan, they were observed driving the jeep back to the McCleans."

As for splitting infinitives, the practice used to be strictly taboo unless the writer wished to stress the adverb for added emphasis. Nowadays, however, the split occurs more often than not, both in conversation and print: To seriously weigh, to quietly observe, to seriously consider, to never fail, to always try. And though split infinitives continue to grate on a few die-hards' consciousness, they've become perfectly acceptable to most of us — to the point, in fact, that infinitives not split now sound unnatural.

Actually, we've been splitting infinitives for so long that it's become the rule than its exception. Take that memorable line from *Star Trek:* "To boldly go where no man has gone before." "Boldly to go where no man has gone before." "To go boldly where no man has gone before." All three variations sound pretty good, though most of us would agree that splitting the infinitive here lends more pace and panache to the word imagery.

It's no longer a case, then, of never breaking the rules of grammar, usage, and style as much as keeping up with our mother tongue's breakneck evolution, always attempting to write with immediacy, vitality, and verve.

"A living stream," is how E. B. White describes the turbulent course of language, "shifting, changing, receiving new strength from a thousand tributaries, losing old forms in the backwaters of time."

Humorist Dave Barry portrayed the mishmash of modern idiom in his own wacky way: "A rich verbal tapestry woven together from the tongues of the Greeks, the Latins, the Angles, the Klaxtons, the Celtics, the 76ers, and many other ancient peoples, all of whom had severe drinking problems." It just seems that way sometimes.

But, you get the point.

Like Barry, we should just relax and enjoy our wonderful language, reveling in words that sing and dance and change colors like chameleons before our eyes. Our delight in innovation and constant change should evidence itself in our writing, because writing and people are most ingratiating when they don't take themselves too seriously. And like people who aren't comfortable with themselves, writing that takes itself too seriously tends to make others uncomfortable as well.

Lighten Up

Self-conscious, pedantic prose is usually boring stuff, often resulting in the worst thing that can happen to its primly precise perpetrators: being ignored. Make that the third-worst thing.

The second-worst thing is to be laughed at when you're not trying to be funny, as in the case of a *New York Times* reporter who revealed, "A hospital official said he expected about 20 percent of the municipal hospital nurses to be Filipino by next year." (For his next trick, will he make them Italian?)

The worst thing, by far, the *worst* thing is to appear dumb in print. Some rules of usage and grammar have been broken to the point of widespread acceptance, but you can't break other rules without seeming careless or lazy. Tarot decks, for instance, contain Hanged Man cards; hung men are found in porno flicks.

Punctuation and quotation marks must be positioned properly. Subjects and predicate verbs ("a *host* of amenities *includes...*") must agree with their objects, as must time, person, and tense, pronouns and antecedents. Dangling, misplaced, and squinting modifiers should not provide chuckles, discomfort, or uncertainty in the minds of readers, for this comic relief comes at the expense of your credibility.

Hard-core grammarians hearing Billy Joel's hit song, "This Night," for the hundredth time still mouth "me" when he croons "It's only you and *I*..."

Helen Reddy is also grammatically wrong, though melodiously dead-on, when she sings, "You and me against the world..."

A four-color, full-bleed ad in *The New York Times Magazine* peddling Fifth Avenue condos distinguished itself with a misplaced apostrophe in the opening sentence of its pricey text: "There are still some New Yorker's who understand the difference." How many dollars worth of credibility do you suppose that typo lopped off the ad?

No matter how forgiving your readers, don't test their patience with wrong grammar and punctuation. It's strictly a no-win preposition when you do. (Good catch! You knew I meant *proposition*.)

Counting both active and passive voice, verbs can express 24 different time-relationships. You won't need most of them, but use the ones you do correctly. Don't appear wrong in print to your readers regardless of how many writers have made the same mistakes before you. Their wrongs don't make you right. You'll still be wrong.

Take the perennially abused verb "comprise." There are as many readers who know as those who don't that the whole comprises its parts, not vice versa. And as many writers who don't know this grammatical rule as there are readers. One of them is an Associated Press reporter who noted in a story appearing in the (South Carolina) *Island Packet:* "The top 10 is comprised of four boxers, three golfers, two auto racing drivers, and one basketball player." ("The top 10 comprises four…")

Still, sacrificing free-flowing narrative for the pure sake of rigidly proper grammar is a bigger mistake. Fledgling writers tend to self-consciously rein in their copy to the point of stultification. Quarrel not with technical precision achieved at the expense of severing the human connection that touches an emotional chord, flips a mental light switch, plucks a moral nerve, tugs a heartstring, or tickles a funny bone.

These are ends difficult to attain with rigid prose that stiffens into rigor mortis on the printed page or electronic screen. Better to go for the emotional connection.

Be Yourself

Filling your newsletter by each relentless deadline is a feat in itself, but that worthy end should not be your only aspiration. Having each issue touch, influence, and affect your reader —

that should be your singular goal. And the best way to achieve it is to subordinate *everything* you write to one unyielding objective — engaging, motivating, galvanizing your readers. If organizational communicators don't regularly achieve these objectives, what's the point of what they do?

Above all, then, let your empathy show through what you write.

Above all, then, be yourself when you write.

Let your humor, personality, empathy, charisma — everything that makes you who you are — shine through your words. That's what empathy is, what makes it all-important in organizational communications. It's your sensitivity to the feelings, thoughts, values, and experiences of others that determines whether your message gets through to them.

Connection is what communications is all about — your ability to relate to others. If you can't relate, you won't connect, regardless of how polished your prose.

Some call it personal style, referring not to literary excellence but the individuality of your writing — *you* emerging, becoming clear and distinct in your words. Your readers will respond to this heightened sense of you in your copy, one person relating to another, in thought, feelings, experiences, hopes, beliefs, values.

Another tip on breathing naturalness and spontaneity into your writing: Do what speechwriters do: Read your writing out loud to yourself. *Say* the words as you punch them onto the computer screen. By speaking what you write as you write it, you'll be able to hear the cadence of your words, test their fluidity, feel their movement. If your writing sounds stiff, you can be sure it really is.

Some final advice on making business writing less formal and more personal. Don't write to the whole world. Pick out an individual, someone you know and like, whose opinion you respect, and who likes you back and respects hearing what you have to say. Keep that one person in your mind as you write. Picture him or her reading your words and reacting to them.

That's all you need — one person, one reader at a time — and you'll be on track with everyone else.

CHAPTER 4

OFF WITH A BANG: BUILDING POWERFUL LEADS

It's the opening kick of a football game returned for a touchdown. Or fumbled.

It's what orange juice is to breakfast, the first minutes of a blind date, a salesman's opening remarks.

It sets the tone, lights the stage, greases the skids for everything to follow.

It's the most important part of everything you'll ever write, because if it doesn't work, whatever follows won't matter. It won't get read.

It's your opening paragraph. And enough can't be said about its importance.

Seduction. That's basically what leads are all about — enticing the reader across the threshold of your article — because nothing happens till you get 'em inside. And you literally have only seconds to do it because surveys show that eight out of ten people quit reading an article after the first fifty words.

You have even less time in cyberspace, cautions Linda Aksomitis, on-line writing coach, photojournalist, and published author of 19 fiction and nonfiction titles, including five ebooks. Citing Nielsen NetRatings statistics, she points out that Internet surfers visit the Web for an average of an hour each day but skim through the material they access at a breakneck pace.

"In that hour," says Aksomitis, "the surfer visits an average of 43 web pages and spends about 45 seconds on each page, suggesting that users are interested in skimming over the contents of a page, rather than spending time going in depth.

"This means its very important to keep the reader engaged and get to your point quickly!" she stresses.

Whether achieved with humor, shock, revelation, irreverence, curiosity, novelty, irony, or eloquence, your lead must immediately captivate readers, compel them to continue reading your breathless prose.

Whatever Works

There are no rules for accomplishing this critical end. Well, maybe one: Whatever works. Lead paragraphs can be a single word. Or they can fill the whole page. They can stroll into your readers' consciousness or blast through their walls of indifference.

Leads can stun, amuse, mystify, enthrall, disorient — thoroughly engage — whatever it takes to seize the reader's attention and propel it in the firm grip of your eloquence to the next line, the next paragraph, the next page.

And the next, and the next, until the final spellbinding syllable.

But even if you lose some of your audience halfway through, you will have succeeded partially, perhaps fully, by engrossing them long enough to get your main points across.

And don't feel bad about not hanging onto them until your last honeyed phrase. Typical readers don't finish most articles they begin.

But they do start at the beginning to decide whether the piece merits their attention. And that's where you have to place your best words. Advertising professionals know their prospects' attention must be earned in those crucial first moments between the time they flip one page until they turn the next.

They know they have to succeed immediately. Or not at all.

How often have you finished reading a print ad, then asked yourself, "Why did I *do* that? I don't care about this product!"? The answer is the ad worked — the way your leads must work.

"The lead functions like bail in a trap," points out *Writer's Digest* columnist Art Spikol. "It draws the reader in and occupies him in such a way as to make him unaware that the door by which he entered has closed tightly behind him."

Adcrafters try to blend beguiling copy, evocative graphics, suitable typography, arresting photos or illustrations, and full-bleed color to halt their prospects in mid-flight, making escape unthinkable.

Your task is harder. For you have only the power of your words.

A Repertoire of Leads

Make a habit of studying leads, mentally labeling them as you do, and you'll find yourself lumping them into categories. Your awareness of their differences should impel you to expand your own repertoire of article openers. One you'll encounter often is the "weather report" lead, typified by these examples:

> On a magnificent sunny day in Portland that single-handedly atones for six months of Oregon rain, Dr. Stan James sits in the city's downtown Pioneer Courthouse Square and talks about "nature's mistake": the knee.

o

> It's a dazzling autumn morning, crisp, cloudless and well, "just perfect for looking at buildings," says Jerry Cooper, unlocking his green Jaguar.

o

> On this f/8, 1/125th-of-a-second morning, flat, cloudless light slants down on the five photographers gathered in a bright corner of the spacious Northwest Portland studio.

Start looking for weather report leads and you'll see they're a popular opener, to the point of being overdone. Still, it's an approach that lends a dash of style to otherwise ordinary copy:

On a breezy Yorkshire Sunday morning, you're running 11 miles.

o

"The temperamental spring day can't quite decide what kind of an afternoon it wants to be."

o

Daybreak. A cornfield. Two men in evening clothes. And a seven-foot lizard on a leash.

o

The sun glares over Beverly Hills as...

o

On a misty Friday evening in Chevy Chase, Maryland...

o

On a bright spring morning in the cabin of his...

o

On a gunmetal-gray day, the sky wrapping the land like wet moleskin...

o

The sun is a red ball just starting to climb.

o

On a Tuesday evening ripe with spring…

Borrowing from Fiction

Then there are "narrative" leads (aka "anecdotal," "case history," "prime example," and "scene-setting" openers) borrowed from fiction writers to inject immediate drama into news and feature stories. Here are some examples.

This narrative lead launches an employee magazine profile:

> Chuck Dagman's life and career changed abruptly on a February morning in 1961 when he parachuted into a detonated minefield outside of Metz, France. On that fateful day a dozen years ago he was a young U.S. Army first lieutenant assigned to the elite Tenth Special Forces Group, with his mind set on becoming a career officer.

Here's a narrative lead from a magazine piece on chocoholics:

> A mouthful of broccoli, a mouthful of chocolates. Gulping a spoonful of vegetables, 4-year-old Colleen Kennemore would run around the family dining room table to be rewarded for the feat with a slice of Milky Way. String beans and chocolate, cauliflower and chocolate, asparagus and chocolate. One after the other in a satiating ritual of obedience and reward that would shock the socks off today's nutrition experts.

A narrative lead from a newsletter piece explaining the purpose of corporate profits:

> The sun warm on his back, Sam Smith squinted along the windowsill and brushed on another coat of paint. A soft breeze fanned his face as he dipped his brush back

into the paint can.

"Hey, Dad?"

Sam looked down from his lofty perch on the ladder into the anxious eyes of his son. "What is it, Bill?"

"How do you define 'profit,' Dad?"

Editor Downs Matthews used this narrative lead to launch a similar article in *Exxon USA:*

"Could I ask you a question, sir?"

"Lay it on me, man."

"Could you define the term 'profit'?"

"Oh, wow, man. You can't define Khalil Gibran. Like he's just too much."

"I see. Perhaps this person...Madam, could you define the term 'profit' for me?"

"Profit? Of course, comrade. I have a written definition in my purse. If you'll just hold my bomb."

Here's one from a magazine piece on an immigrant restaurateur:

Juggling several heaping platters of food, waitress Daphna Kunio blurs by, but not fast enough for Ted Papas to miss the grilled cheese sandwiches on two of the plates. "Hold it!" commands Papas. Kunio skids to a halt. "Take 'em back," he orders. "They're overdone." As the waitress knifes back through the noonday crowd, Papas reboards his train of thought.

Another narrative lead from a feature profile on a master violin-maker:

> Tapping, palming, caressing the wood, he literally feels its promise. Peering at the grain as if to memorize it, sensing as much as hearing the strum of the boards between his fingers, he makes his first critical choices — two matching pieces of maple for the back, two of spruce for the top. They will be crucial to the instrument's tonal quality.

What If . . .?

Other types of leads can be as engaging. One of them answers the "What if...?" question:

> If Melody Weir were a city, she'd be San Francisco.

o

> If New England were human instead of geographic, it would have a personality only a mother could love.

o

> If Oliver North were a stock, the word on Wall Street would be "buy."

o

> If Hannibal the Cannibal, the fiendish serial-killer portrayed in *The Silence of the Lambs* were in a California prison, he would be locked up in the Pelican Bay State Prison's Security Housing Unit.

Query Leads

There's also the question lead, disdained by some editors as a limp way to launch articles — advisable only if the query carries enough impact. But it's an opener that gets right to the meat of the subject. A few examples:

What do snowflakes, fingerprints and company printers have in common?

o

What if you were suddenly notified by your friendly neighborhood lending institution that you now had to pay the going interest rate on the home mortgage you took out 15 years ago?

o

What should you do if you have lots of money tied up in bonds that were healthy only a few years ago but are barely breathing now?

o

What's next for advocates of affirmative action and quotas to conquer?

o

What do Nike, the investment firm Grunthal & Company and *Vogue* magazine have in common?

o

What's the difference between a battered short seller and a real bear? The bear knows when it's time to pack it in and go into hibernation.

o

Which is more prone to collapse: the commercial real estate market or a cheese soufflé?

o

Are companies today doing poorly because we're in a recession, or are we in a recession because companies are doing poorly?

o

Advertise lumber like razor blades?

Summing Up Succinctly

The single-word lead, eye-catching in its brevity, is effective because it bluntly sums up the gist of the piece:

Shoestrings.

They come lashed to the American Dream. But only sometimes. More often than not they just snap.

o

Creativity.

They wear the word like epaulets on their collective shoulders. It is their rallying cry, the Holy Grail they pursue, their only product, they insist, and their professional shtick.

o

Slither.

Pets that slip and slide. That don't go bump in the night. That don't mess the rug, scratch the furniture, chase the mail carrier or wake up the neighbors at three in the morning.

o

Meat.

It's the new four-letter word. "Beef," bemoans a National Cattleman's Association brochure, "has become the whipping boy for food faddists, diet-book authors and even some scientists and nutritionists."

Grabber Leads

Particularly powerful openers are "consciousness-altering" leads, so strong they lean off the page to grab you by your lapels:

Justin Rodarte is going to die. He is seven years old and tells you with the calm, unblinking, total certainty of youth, yes, he knows it. Within a year, he thinks.

o

It resembles something out of a Vincent Price movie. Or the Inquisition. A fiendish device to crush bones, perhaps...slowly, methodically, making screaming believers out of heretics.

o

On a cold November Friday two and a half years ago, Randy Huyett boarded Eastern Airlines flight 257 in Raleigh-Durham, N.C.

The jet took off at 9:09 A.M., bound for Atlanta, and landed two hours and 48 minutes later. In Havana.

It had been hijacked.

o

What's the world coming to? One moment you're sitting in your car a block from your office building waiting for the light to turn green. Next thing you know there's a wild man in the front seat with you, perched on the company mail you just picked up at the post office, jamming an ice pick into your ribs, and hollering for you to drive him out of Portland toward the Oregon coast.

You've been kidnapped!

A tamer version of the consciousness-altering lead is the merely "startling" opener, which doesn't clobber but is disconcerting enough to garner attention. A few examples:

The people at Boise Cascade in Wallula did an interesting thing in pursuit of product quality a year ago. They got rid of their quality control inspectors. And gave the job to everyone else at the mill.

o

Jo Underwood, Olive Hartz, Marlys McAfee, and Cecile Thompson talk a lot. And they tend to repeat themselves. But that's what they get paid to do. And they do it exceedingly well.

Between the four of them they say, "Good morning"
and "Good afternoon" some 1,200 times a day, which is
the average number of calls that come through their
telephone exchange board daily.

o

David Knapp enjoyed a stroke of good luck last July:
one of his dealerships was robbed.

o

As far as the phone company is concerned, St.
Stanislaus Church doesn't exist.

o

"I'm surprised I don't glow in the dark," Cricket
Schernbeck says, recalling his 30 years working in
hospital radiology.

Analogy Leads

Also effective are analogy leads, which link similarities in
distinctly different items to make a point:

Some big business deals are like jellyfish: as dangerous
dead or alive.

o

Like encircled wagon-train pioneers heartened by
approaching cavalry, beleaguered Northwest
aluminum companies hope the long-awaited relief
arrives in time.

o

Selling your business is like watching your kids leave home. It's what you've been working toward all these years, but when it happens, it's hard to let go.

o

America's crisis of leadership is like trying to start a stalled car on a highway.

We can't start the engine because the battery is dead, but we can't charge the battery because the engine won't run.

o

Corporate divisions are a lot like in-laws. Some get along fine, while many others can't stand one another. Yet, companies, like people, tend to benefit and prosper when all in the family interact and communicate.

o

The American economy used to resemble a fallen soufflé: firm around the edges and soft in the middle.

Sheer Eloquence

Another spellbinder is the eloquent lead, so poetically evocative you can't help but dig down for more. This one parts the curtain on the profile of a company town:

The river dominates the land and the lives of the people on it. They speak her name softly here, possessively, almost tenderly, as if she were a person rather than a body of water: Miramichi.

Here's a poetic lead from a land developer's newsletter:

> It is a place made for the dawn. And the blood-red
> sunsets of the Carolina low country. A place where
> ocean and river lean on the land, and the morning mist
> cloaks meadows of wildflowers until a copper sky
> reveals the mystery and enchantment below.

From a Hawaii private club community brochure:

> Above, Maui's green and gold mountains tower over
> sculptured fairways and emerald greens. Below, pale
> surf washes the crystal sands of Kaanapali Beach. And
> beyond, in Kealaikahiki Channel, the islands of Lanai
> and Molokai drift in a boundless sea.

From an oil company newsletter:

> Bligh Reef. Exxon Valdez. These names now stir a
> graphic image of the giant supertanker grounding on
> the rocks, rupturing, releasing 10 million gallons of oil
> into the pristine marine environment of Prince William
> Sound. That tragedy impacts not only Exxon and the
> residents of Alaska, but the entire oil industry and the
> fate of future energy development.

Aside from immediately involving the reader, captivating leads do some work in revealing what the piece is about while convincing the reader to stick around for the finish.

But don't dawdle too long in setting your hook. Then pull your readers along by keeping the line taut while you continue to build interest.

Be sure, though, they're securely hooked before getting into necessary specifics and details.

Make 'em Laugh

Because everyone loves humor, which can be as hard to pull off as eloquence, the funny lead can be highly effective. It doesn't have to be a knee-slapper — mildly amusing will do — because most of us welcome both writing and people that don't take themselves too seriously.

Three frothy examples from *The New York Times*:

> They went that-a-away. No, that-a-away. Well, then, maybe that-a-way.

o

> Call me, Ishmael. We'll do lunch.

o

> Staring head-on into the face of an angry rattlesnake is one of those things you are not supposed to do and you know it. The thinking brain tells itself, "Why don't you get out of the way, fool?" while the primal brain resorts to a simple, "Aaargh!"

Here's a light one from *Forbes:*

> The talent agent, his yacht capsized, is drowning at sea. Suddenly he is rescued and taken ashore by a man-eating shark. Professional courtesy, of course.

From a community club newsletter:

> In a world filled with fruitcakes — six million pounds of it a year — Paul Parker finds refuge at Harbour Town. Here, enfolded by the natural beauty of Hilton Head, he eases the pressures of running Claxton

Bakery, one of the largest fruitcake-producing companies in the country.

Another from *Forbes* magazine:

An oilman dies, goes to heaven and approaches God. "Lord," he says, "will the natural gas glut ever go away?" God thinks a moment and says, "Yes, but not in my lifetime."

One from the *Business Journal:*

I spent last weekend with 685 good-looking, physically fit women. It was exhausting. But great. As one of a handful of men attending the first state-sponsored women's leadership conference on health and fitness...

Two from an employee newsletter:

We're at Weaver Street Market in Carroboro, N.C, my wife and I, and a woman with a smile that doesn't move is pushing a bite-size piece of pizza at me, "Soy," she says. "Tofu." *Gesundheit*, I think.

o

One sure way to meet people in the Zebulon facility is to ask them about their laundry. That's true at least for Jan Taylor, who is responsible — among other duties — for collecting, laundering, and returning more than 2,000 production uniforms and lab coats per week.

Some Things Aren't Funny

Watch it, though. Humor is hard to pull off. It's one of the first things to jump off the page or screen and bite an editor — or just lie there and die — because one person's guffaw is another's groan.

What's more, most communicators and their bosses are deathly afraid of humor in print, because they don't understand and thus don't trust it. That's why so little humor appears in organizational publications, except unintentionally, as in this hilarious moment in an otherwise bland Hawaiian resort newsletter. A cover story detailing the enjoyment of guests referenced a 500-pound marlin hooked by a mainland visitor: "She declined putting it on the menu," related the newsletter writer, "and opted to mount it instead."

Yet, handled well, humor can be tremendously effective by cutting through the methodical sterility of many organizational communications.

Some advice, however, on employing humor in business writing: Don't make it hurtful to others. Turn it inward instead. Most successful business and political humor is self-deprecating. Keep in mind, too, that humor is inappropriate in serious situations, especially if it's wielded by individuals responsible for fixing the problem — not making light of it.

And if corporate managers suggest that humor has no place in organizational publications, refer them to that most austere of business bibles, the *Harvard Business Review,* and its popular cartoons.

Your Leads *Must* Succeed

There are many other kinds of leads, but you get the idea. Identifying the variety available can remind you that their primary objective is to get readers *into* the article before they flip the page.

If that doesn't happen, the remainder of what you write — however provocative or informative or entertaining — won't matter. If your lead doesn't snag their attention as it floats or darts by, they'll never know what they missed.

So be paranoid about your leads. No matter how long the piece that follows or how little time you're given to tell your story, don't proceed on the journey without being fully satisfied with the first few steps. Only when you're happy with your lead — no, when you're ecstatic about it — should you move along.

There are those who advise getting on with your writing, not getting hung up on beginnings. Get it all down first, they urge, and fix it up later. But many writers can't work that way. Because the lead is so critical to the piece, they won't continue with the word-structure they're crafting until they have something rock-solid to build on — that riveting first word, first sentence, first paragraph, first page.

For them, the lead is a superb beginning, from which everything else flows naturally.

And when they're done, they try to loop back to their perfect beginning, neatly lassoing the whole bundle of words into a cohesive package, imparting a feeling of completion to the piece. At least that's the intention.

Striving for the ideal beginning and ending should be reflexive, regardless of how deadly dull the copy may be in-between.

CHAPTER 5

THE FEATURE STORY: GRAB HOLD, HANG ON

These opening lines of an article about opening lines of another sort are as typical of a feature lead as you're likely to find:

"Herman Hupfeld."

"I beg your pardon?"

That's what she'll probably say.

Then repeat the name: "Herman Hupfeld."

And start humming the tune from *Casablanca,* the one the piano player always sings when Rick tells him, "Play it, Sam." *Da da da da da **da.** Da da da da da **da**. Da da da da da da. Da da da da da da da **daaa**. Da da da **da**.*

You got her attention now, boy!

Then say the name again: "Herman Hupfeld." Pause three beats before adding, "He wrote it. You know, *As Time Goes By.* From the Humphrey Bogart movie."

This is the critical point, when she says, "Is that so, you silver-tongued devil?"

Or you say, "Wait, don't go…"

Wait! Don't *you* go, gentle reader. Sorry to lead you on like that.

I did it to hammer home a point about feature articles: The beginning always justifies the end. For you must get your readers into the piece, snag their attention in the few moments before they restlessly move. If not, you've lost them forever.

This narrative lead from *Investment Vision* succeeds. Though it takes a while getting to where it's going, we go along willingly because it's fun:

> A-WOP-BOP-A-LOO-MOP-ALOP-BAM-BOOM. It's Saturday night in Austin, Texas, and the joint is jumping. Little Richard, *the* Little Richard, his trademark pompadour glistening like the silver studs on his black jumpsuit, his teeth and wide eyes flashing like a televangelist's, is at the piano, prancing and stomping, leaping and crouching. He's pounding the keys so wildly he's got bankers and accountants and lawyers — guys whose pulses rarely race unless the cash register's ringing — dancing on tabletops so wantonly it seems that multiple heart attacks are imminent.
>
> A profile on Little Richard, right? Wrong! And the magazine writer dangles his readers for another long paragraph before letting them in on exactly what the piece is about:
>
> Some 700 revelers are jammed into the Four Seasons Hotel ballroom this November evening in 1989. Many of the men were fraternity brothers a quarter-century ago at the University of Texas; many of the women were sorority sisters who married their boyfriends. The alumni are here to worship at the altar of their rock and roll god, but also to genuflect before another Richard, their fraternity's "Tau Man of the Year": Richard E. Rainwater, the legendary Texas dealmaker.

Granted, the build-up above is a tad long, but it drives home the point that softer (non-news story) leads come in every size, shape, and style.

Because feature writers don't have the lure of "hard" news to keep the attention of readers, they must rely instead on their skill with words. Let's look at a few more opening grafs of feature articles.

Note how each lead differs from the others. And let's see where each of them takes us.

Consider this one from *Manhattan, Inc.*:

> Just before noon on May 9, 1990, Robert L. Dilenschneider is standing in his spacious office on the eleventh floor of the Graybar Building, getting ready to go to lunch. Outside, police cars line Lexington Avenue. They are there to control an angry crowd. These people are pointing up at the building and yelling, "SHAME! SHAME! SHAME!"
>
> Dilenschneider knows they are out there. If he were to push aside his dark blue curtains and crack the window, he might even hear them. But he does not, because, although they are there because of him, he still does not think he has made a mistake.

Here's one from the *Washington Post Magazine*:

> Fashion, like the Lord, moves in mysterious ways. Women cry out for "basic" clothes they can wear in "real" life. You know, blazers and skirts — nothing faddish or trendy, please. After all, at today's prices, clothes have to be long-lived investments. Then along comes a 21-year-old designer who makes kiddie-colored dresses — expensive dresses — based on the Crayolas of our youth, and the ladies line up, waving their charge cards. Did we say "basic"? We didn't mean it! Honest!

And one from *Lear's* magazine:

> When I heard on a newscast that the shifting earth around the San Andreas Fault had uncovered the site of a prehistoric village somewhere in Southern California, I found it hard to believe. But I put in a call to the distinguished archaeologist in charge, Professor Theodore L. Guber, asking him if there was any truth to the story, and to my surprise, there was. "I'm off tomorrow to begin the dig," he said. "Come along if you like."

From the *The Wall Street Journal:*

> They bought and sold homes like traders in the pork-belly pit.

> It was the 1980s, and hundreds of thousands of baby boomers, two-income couples with ready access to credit, were buying New York real estate. Frenzied buyers bid against one another even for small, dark fifth-floor walkups, terrified they might be snatched away by someone smarter.

> Buying a home was the ultimate investment: tax advantages, sure appreciation — and, incidentally, a place to sleep. Many buyers never considered actually settling down in these places. They were pit slops on the way to bigger and better.

Each writer has crafted an attention-grabbing lead. Now, with the reader hooked and snugly in tow, it's time for what magazine editors call the "nut" graf — newspaper lingo for the feature writer's equivalent of the news reporter's five W's, providing a quick sketch of the informational terrain the writer intends to tread, allowing the reader to decide whether to keep reading or move on.

A Light Shining Down

Call it a flashlight shining down into the article. (The metaphor is *New Yorker* writer John McPhee's.) That's what the nut graf should do after it has hooked the reader: Illuminate the editorial ground the writer is inviting readers to tread. With the information provided them in the nut graf, they can to choose to explore further, or not, based on this snapshot of what is to follow. This snapshot is the nut graf.

But the writer must allow readers to decide for themselves early on. Stringing them along indefinitely, regardless of how entertaining the writing, can be irritating, causing the reader to lose patience and move on. The flashlight must reveal the editorial path fairly soon after the lead has done its job.

Let's revisit a few of the stories we started above. This is the nut graf comprising the third paragraph of the *Manhattan, Inc.* piece. Here, in five sentences, is what this feature story is all about: The world's largest public relations firm and the blockbuster challenge taken on by its under-fire-to-boost-earnings president, Bob Dilenschneider.

> For the last four years the 46-year-old Dilenschneider has been president and CEO of Hill and Knowlton, the world's largest public relations firm. He has advised American Airlines, IBM, Eastman Kodak, PepsiCo, Chase Manhattan, and the Rockefeller Group. He has turned down requests for PR help from Manuel Noriega and organized crime. In March, under heavy pressure from Hill and Knowlton's British owner, Martin Sorrell's WPP Group, to make the firm more profitable, he said yes to a new client: Pro-life bishops.

The *Washington Post Magazine s* nut graf spells out the article's content in this fashion:

> The three young talents featured here — 21-year-old Christian Francis Roth, 28-year-old Malaysia-born Zang

Toi and 35-year-old Gemma Kahng from Korea — are among the latest crop. If their ideas and garments catch on, their names will soon be seen in department stores, they will spin off less-expensive lines of clothing, and, maybe later, they will have their own line of fragrance or sunglasses.

And here's the "nut" of *Wall Street Journal* staff reporter Cynthia Crossen's piece, comprising the third and fourth paragraphs: A look at the changing attitude of baby boomers on real estate investments in the '90's:

Today, with housing prices falling, many of those same people are finding that putting down roots can be an economic as well as an emotional decision. After years of thinking of houses as investments first and homes second, a generation is reordering those priorities.

These days, when baby boomers buy a home, they often are really buying a *home*.

Mining the Editorial Vein

In the case of *Lear's* writer Peter Feibleman, his lead paragraph also serves as the nut graf in news story style as he makes it clear right off exactly where he will be taking his readers. But not until his fifth paragraph does Feibleman reveal the amusing editorial vein he will mine throughout his piece, namely the professor's greater awe of movie stars than of the archaeological digs near their homes.

Which brings us to a third distinguishing characteristic of feature writing: the "angle" or editorial peg on which each story is hung, namely its unifying theme.

From the pivotal lead to the nut graf and throughout the entire organic structure with its unraveling skein of anecdotes, quotes, expositive and narrative segments, facts, figures, and summarizing paragraphs, everything in the feature story should flow naturally and cohesively from the writer's approach to the article.

Because the "angle" is so critical to the final treatment of the piece, like a rising soufflé in a low-temperature oven it must be given enough time to evolve effortlessly and develop fully.

Narrative Glue

Let's go back to a couple of the features we've been tracking.

First, Peter Feibleman's piece from *Lear's* is anecdotal throughout, reading almost like fiction, which is why his use of the first person seems natural here. As the writer recounts his visit with Professor Guber and their ensuing conversations about archeology, the professor's amusing infatuation with show biz becomes obvious. It is the glue Feibleman uses to holds his narrative together. Early on, he recounts:

> I knelt there a moment, awestruck. "You mean to tell me there's a prehistoric village under Barbra Streisand's house?"

> "Oh, goodness no," he said. "The ruin is 200 miles from here. I just thought I'd take in something interesting while I was in the neighborhood. If you've seen one prehistoric village, you've seen them all."

Several paragraphs later, Guber asks, "I wonder where Tom Cruise lives?" Four paragraphs later, Guber asks excitedly, "I wonder if that man standing by the exit is Jack Nicholson." Five paragraphs later, Guber's infatuation surfaces again:

> Pulling himself up from the floor, Professor Guber cocked his head a few degrees to the left. "Palm Springs is only 10 or 20 miles from here...it's conceivable that the ruin extends that far...I wonder if he lives in Palm Springs."

"Who?"

"Jack Nicholson." he said.

And so Feibleman stitches his story securely together with the unifying thread of the professor's infatuation with celebrity. It is his "angle."

In her *Wall Street Journal* look at how baby boomers are reordering their priorities by regarding their estate purchases as homes first and investments second, Cynthia Crossen makes her case with a dozen or so authoritative quotes interspersed with supporting data.

"It's a lot more important for me to find a place that's comfortable than one that will pay me a big dividend in a few years," Crossen quotes the first boomer, echoing her nut graf. "I'm certainly not going to raise a family in this apartment and grow old and retire here," remarks the second boomer. "I wish someone had said to me, 'No, no, no, don't buy until you're ready to stay for a long time.' "

Crossen proceeds to buttress her thesis with the opinions of a professor of architecture, following with a quote from a third disgruntled boomer, who disdains the 1,000-square-foot Queens apartment in which she grew up, "I wouldn't even rent it now as a *pied-à-terre*. For my parents it was suitable. But we're brats. We were trained to be brats." Crossen then goes on to quote a Realtor, a trade publication editor, a real-estate marketing president, and finally three more baby boomers.

Relax, therefore, in the knowledge that feature articles take on countless forms. You needn't mimic what anyone else has done. Structure your own as you see fit, working with the material you've been able to pull together. There are no hard-and-fast rules, so long as you hold your readers until the end. Some stories are so interesting they seem to tell themselves. Others need much more of your reporting and writing skills.

A word of caution though. Lack of any structure whatsoever will be obvious to your readers and will try their patience, even if you've chosen a promising subject and researched it well.

Make no mistake, good feature articles do have structure, which may be hidden, but it must be there for the feature article to have unity and cohesion, even though it appears effortlessly assembled.

Consider Them Doorknobs

Vital to the seamless structure of successful feature articles are their *transitions*. Regard these interlocking words and phrases as doorknobs, if you will, convenient handles for readers to grasp, leading the way from sentence to sentence and to each succeeding paragraph. Transitions guide the reader from one thought to another — from each tidy packet of information to the next — showing the way through each door until every threshold is crossed in the smooth passage from opening line to closing sentence.

Art Spikol compares awkward or nonexistent transitions to bumps in the road of the reader's consciousness:

> One sentence you're one place, the next sentence you're someplace else — and either you don't know what you're doing there or you're painfully aware of how you got there: choppy writing. Smooth transitions, on the other hand, get readers to the next subject without any awareness that the subject has changed at all; they feel that they're reading a logical extension of the previous thought. And if you've ever wondered what makes an article just plod along instead of reading quickly, chances are the article consists of paragraphs stacked one on top of another with no transitions of any kind, rough or smooth.

Often the simplest way to move readers from sentence to sentence, paragraph to paragraph, thought to thought, is with an "and" or a "but," contrary to the lingering admonitions of your grammar school teachers. Other common connectives are "or," "nor," "although," "also," "too," "then," "however," and "furthermore." Be wary, though, of their overuse, which signals an unimaginative writer.

Much worse, however, is for you to halt your readers in mid-sentence, wondering if they're still mired in one thought or on their way to the next. Make it clear to them as they navigate from sentence to sentence, paragraph to paragraph, thought to thought, exactly where they stand in your parade of information and ideas.

When prose propels us from one image to another, the passages seem natural, perfectly logical, moving us fluidly past the changing scenery. Next time you read a well-crafted piece that impels you from line to line without any mental bumps or disjointed pauses, examine how the writer carried you along so effortlessly. It's the best way to learn how to do it yourself.

Transitions, then, are vital as they couple sentences and paragraphs firmly and efficiently into a well-oiled train of thought.

Tell and Show

Another component of engrossing features is vivid imagery. Without a news "hook" to grasp the reader's attention, human-interest pieces demand much more than an orderly procession of facts, figures, information, and quotes. The feature writer must make the material come alive, not by merely relating the pertinent facts but by immersing the readers' senses in the narrative. By making them see, hear, smell, and touch everything they need to experience to feel whatever it is you want them to feel.

As a student of writing, you may have been told "*Show*, don't tell." Heed that wise directive, but change it to "Show *and* tell." Words aren't worth much unless they ignite images in the mind and imagination. Those images come alive in the reader's consciousness through evocative sights, sounds, smells, and colors regaled on the printed page.

Take this weather-report lead that draws the curtain on a piece on 'garbologists":

First light comes grudgingly after a night of grumbling thunder. Dawn leaks in wet and muggy, dragging a day typical of a very untypical Portland summer. Steam rises from the waiting garbage.

It is 6:02 when Larry Littrell cases his International Cargostar to a halt in front of Riverdale School on Southwest Military Road and Breyman Avenue. He greets his early morning rider with an economy of words that suits the hour.

The diesel truck lurches forward again. Terry Pepiot, 23, Littrell's loader for the day, dangles nonchalantly from one side. Both men wear baseball caps. Pepiot's visor is pulled low, trapping smoke from the cigarette seldom out of his mouth, blurring his features. A button hanging from the side of Littrell's black cap reads "CONSERVE ENERGY: Do Everything As Slow As You Can." Another button, pinned above the bill, asks, "Are You Stoned or Just Stupid?" Pepiot says he found the cap and buttons in the garbage. Otherwise, the two men are nondescript in flannel and khaki shirts, faded jeans and work boots. The jeans and shirts testify to one of the job's basic hazards. A river of Tide will never wash them clean.

It will be a while before Littrell, 34, warms to the subject at hand. But Pepiot, filling in for Littrell's usual partner, never does. "It all looks the same to me," he says on his second morning of doing what Littrell has done every working morning for the past 16 years. To Pepiot, the task at hand is just a job. To Littrell, it's his life's work.

"How you feelin', Mr. Garbage man?" "Down in the dumps."

"How's business?" "Pickin up!"

The nut graf follows, explaining the article's pungent focus:

Garbage. More than just waste and refuse, it is the smörgåsbord of your life laid out for the world to see — as if the world cared.

Garnish with Anecdotes

So you must tell, and you must *show,* if possible, with anecdotes, revealing depictions of events that nail the points you want to convey. Plumb, therefore, for provocative details during your interviews. Ask questions that will provide you with descriptive embellishment and color. Ask: *What* did you think when you heard the sound? *When* did you realize you were in trouble? *Where* were you when the earthquake hit? *How* did you get free? *Why* did you go back? *What* were you feeling?

Anecdotes are worth the patient, diligent digging, for they are the lamps that flood the landscapes of your narrative. Whether telling or showing, skilled writers bathe their readers in a wash of particulars. They use details — a foamy froth of details — to lather their images into shining, vibrant relief.

In United Airlines' in-flight magazine, Chris Barnett launched into his profile of show biz agent Leigh Steinberg with a fact-laden lead that provided immediate insight into his subject:

It is 11 AM and Leigh Steinberg has just finished his hour-long morning ritual — pedaling 50 miles on a vintage stationary Schwinn on his sundeck and tearing through 30 daily newspapers and magazines. Now, fresh from a shower, wearing cutoffs, sandals and a Golden Gear Saloon T-shirt, a boyish-looking Steinberg curls up in a chair in his living room wallpapered with football posters, pops open a Diet Dr. Pepper and is ready to work. I'm wondering to myself, "Is this really the most successful sports lawyer in America, or is he some New Age Huck Finn?"

Note how the animated imagery in Peter Carlson's lead catapults you into his *Washington Post Magazine* piece on D.C.'s National Zoological Park:

The veterinarian approached cautiously as the bongo watched warily. The vet, Lyndsay Phillips, wore jeans, sneakers, a turquoise sport shirt and a ratty brown National Zoo jacket. He was armed with a pole tipped with a needle full of anesthetic. The bongo, a 16-month-old male named Nekuru, was a 350-pound African antelope with white pin stripes running up his brown coat, and a ridge of spiked hair silting along his backbone like a punk-rock haircut. He was armed with two foot-long horns.

This *Northwest Magazine* feature story on veterinarians similarly springs to life with an image-crammed narrative lead:

The walls are antiseptic white, the examining table stainless steel, the patient bright green. Animal health technician Julie Nielsen needs both hands and considerable shoulder muscle to hold down a 4-foot iguana named Smog while veterinarian Tye Wood peers into its bleeding mouth. Wood doesn't have to ask the lizard to say aaaah. The olive jaws gape wide. Nielsen tightens her grip. "We get more scratches from iguanas than from cats," she remarked. "I call 'em lizard lacerations." The scars have faded from Wood's left cheek where a python buried its fangs a couple of years ago. "Pythons don't have the mellow disposition of boa constrictors," offers Wood, whose studious look masks a wry sense of humor. "Boas are the golden retrievers of the snake world."

ADWEEK writer Judith Newman introduces the subject of her article in similarly descriptive fashion:

Today, shifting restlessly in a creaky, straight-backed chair, he wears dusty, black pants, sneakers unevenly laced and a pink, preppy shirt that remembers long, long ago, a visit from an iron — it looks like his mother tried to make him presentable, and gave up.

Gather enough details and the story writes itself, as this lead paragraph from an *Esquire* profile of Jerry Lewis evidences. It is filled with sights, sounds, smells that stirs the reader's senses:

The line for Jerry's final night at the Las Vegas Hilton winds like a polyester Chinese dragon well beyond the gaming tables, past the "WIN A CADILLAC!" slot machine, all the way to the Benihana entrance. The scents of newly minted silver-dollar tokens and draft beer mingle in the mechanically cooled air to form a bouquet of glass-chiller and chlorine.

Similarly, this evocative detail-laden lead could only have resulted from the writer visiting her subject in his office. What she saw there was striking and germane enough to the heart of the article to form its picturesque opener:

Buffaloes thunder across posters, pose for bumper stickers and glower from coffee mugs in Frank Popper's crowded office at Rutgers University in New Jersey. There is even a sack of dried buffalo droppings. "Genuine Virgin Buffalo Chips," the label reads. "Pioneer Fertilizer and Fuel. Not for Microwave Ovens. Contents Public Domain."

Particulars Breathe Life

Go where people live, work, and play. The natural richness you'll extract from these seminal settings will breathe warmth, honesty, and genuine emotion into your stories.

See how the two-paragraph lead below, simply penned and starkly vivid, flows effortlessly, seamlessly into the eloquent nut graf that directly follows:

> Dyersville, Iowa, Aug. 11 — The cars come throughout the day, churning clouds of dust as they bump over the gravel roads, carrying passengers bound like pilgrims for the little baseball diamond cut from the green sea of corn. They arrive, as many as 1,000 a week, bringing their bats and balls and video cameras and waiting in line to take their cuts at the plate and run the bases and handle grounders in the infield of what was a movie set — the diamond built in 1988 by Universal pictures for the film "Field of Dreams." For two summers now, since the movie was released, the little ball field has grown into a popular, if peculiar, tourist attraction, demonstrating not only the way life sometimes imitates art, but the power of art as prophecy.

Make Lists

Details — piled upon details — bring stories to vibrant life and make them work. As a feature writer, develop the habit of collecting particulars. Long lists of them. More details than you'll ever use but assuring you of having everything you'll need when you begin writing your story. Jot down every fact and figure you encounter while researching your articles.

Even use a camera to preserve your recollection of scenes, events, landscapes, colors, textures, nuances, and features. Far removed from the scene, back at your desk, however long later, it will make the writing so much easier.

Painstakingly record all the unusual and interesting sights, sounds, colors, smells, the atmosphere, mood and "feel" of the people and places you encounter while digging for your stories. Note brand names, for instance, in describing what you see: "a crumpled pack of Camels," "Reeboks that look like they never ran a race," "trail-scuffed L.L. Bean loafers," "a dingy car-keyed '92 Honda Accord."

Indeed, both heaven and the devil are in the details.

Do your subjects have distinguishing characteristics? How are they dressed? Do plaques, scrolls, framed photos, memorabilia decorate their offices? Are their desks fastidiously tidy or rumpled like slept-in beds? Is any artwork hung on the walls? Does a certain decor dominate? Much ego usually attaches to personal statements and other manifestations of self in a working environment. An executive, for instance, with the race numbers of seventeen marathons tacked to a cork-board behind her desk has an obvious conversational button to push.

Make notes on physical features, mannerisms, attire, incongruities in physical settings — anything to help illuminate the individual's temperament, work-habits, sense of humor, lifestyle, career motivations, or whatever interesting asides that might help you paint a clearer, more interesting word portrait of your subject.

Whenever you're interrupted during an interview, keep your eyes and your pen moving while your interviewee is tending to other things. You won't be sorry for recording facts you don't use, but often you'll wish you'd noted a few more specifics while you had the chance.

Use the Time Well

Do *not*, however, furiously scribble down everything the interviewee tells you. Try to capture worthwhile quotes verbatim — record them if you can — but if you're only being told what you already know, or you're confident you can paraphrase the conversation later, put your time to better use.

During conversationally barren moments, note your your own thoughts and feelings about what you're seeing and hearing. Or jot down a few questions pertinent to what's developing in the conversation so you don't forget to ask them before your time is up.

Good feature writers often ask questions to which they already know the answer — not necessarily to verify facts or information but in the hope of getting more-readable quotes. Strong statements coupled with revealing anecdotes and strong quotes make for engrossing feature stories.

If you think an interviewee might be able to rephrase his thoughts a bit more clearly, ask him to do just that. Preface your request by bestowing a compliment: "That's interesting. I've never heard it put quite that way before." Then ask for an elaboration on the thought just expressed. Be confident you'll get it.

It's worth a try because there's a rule in feature writing that says the words you put between quotation marks must be extraordinary. In news stories just the facts matter, regardless how ordinarily they're stated. In a feature story, readers expect something special, if not outstanding.

Less than powerful quotes only bleed energy from your piece. Paraphrase the tepid remarks — count on most of what you get being bland, if necessary — just don't make it a quote. Unlike news reporters concerned with accuracy and proper attribution, feature writers exercise the right to omit quotes entirely if they don't measure up.

Or they energize and empower their stories with a profusion of them if they encounter a source that proves to be a mother lode of erudition and wit. It's the writer's call entirely, based on the quality of the material culled from interviews.

Prove it to yourself next time you encounter what you consider to be a compelling feature story. Decide whether every quote in the piece warrants the distinction of wearing the heraldic marks, whether the quote-marks do, indeed, signal readers that something significant their way comes.

For if that promise isn't kept, the resulting disappointment will erode readers' esteem for the writer and their regard for the piece.

Inject Imagery

Skillful feature writers also imbue their stories with richness and vibrancy through the use of picturesque metaphors and colorful similes — nuggets and bursts of word-imagery in the form of descriptive phrases that depict scenes in vivid detail.

With feature stories you are permitted — encouraged, in fact — to be creative with your figures of speech. Instead of a woman's neck being "delicate," it might "curve like a bird taking wing." Shadows can resemble "stalking gray cats." Angular features can be like "water flowing over pebbles in a stream." A man's face might be "as rumpled as the tweed jacket he wears." His glance could be a "gleam of mineral blue."

Two lovers might "cling like Velcro." Instead of a voice sounding tough or faint, rough or reassuring, it could feel like "steel wrapped in silk," or seem to "drift in from a great distance," or "grate like sheets of sandpaper rasped together," or "feel warm and comforting as summer sun."

Here's how a *Weyerhaeuser Today* writer conveyed an employee's weariness:

> "It's still unbelievable," says the mill manager exhaustedly, like a prizefighter who can't believe he must answer one more bell.

Rather than calling a man "thin," national columnist Anna Quindlen pictured him "narrow as an exclamation point." In another column, Quindlen told of a big-eyed boy "clutching a notebook as if it were his heart."

A magazine writer painted this portrait of a seventy-one-year-old marathoner:

A whip-lean greyhound of a man, Davies looks as though he belongs by the sea. Under chalk-white hair, his aquiline features are sharp enough to slice butter. The unswerving gaze impales with raw intensity.

A *New York Times* reporter likened psychologist Oliver Sacks' facial hair to an "implacable gray tide of beard that recalls both the marble sages of Athenian sculpture and the guitarist Jerry Garcia of the Grateful Dead."

Bill Bryson painted this kinetic picture of a high-energy novelist:

Jeffrey Archer doesn't so much walk into a room as bound in. Boyish, good-looking, impeccably dressed in a Jaeger suit and fitter than any 50-year-old has a right to be, he sweeps into the living room of his London penthouse with its wraparound view of the River Thames and the Houses of Parliament, shakes hands with a vigor that suggests he has just stepped out of a very large battery charger and plunks himself comfortably, but restlessly, on one of the room's many plush sofas. Even in repose he gives the impression of an engine with the idle set a little too high.

A newsletter writer depicts his CEO during a lull in the conversation as "staring at the silence around him."

In a magazine profile, a Greek restaurateur is depicted with "an accent thick enough to fricassee" while "his teeth below a flourishing black mustache sparkle like Carpathian coral in the Mediterranean sun."

Consider these four examples of vivid word-imagery from Robert B. Parker's novel, *Perchance to Dream:*

The sunshine was as empty as a headwaiter's smile.

o

His grin had all the warmth of a pawnbroker examining your mother's diamond.

o

She approached me with enough sex appeal to stampede a business men's lunch.

o

The room was as charming as a heap of coffee grounds.

Again, though, too much editorial seasoning in corporate journalism can be as noticeable as none at all. Yet an occasional dash can and should flavor relentlessly tepid prose with sorely needed body and zest.

Tie It Up Neatly

Finally, close the loop on your story. Complete the cycle from beginning to end. Hearken your departing words back to the lead to impart a sense of unity and completion to the piece. It isn't always necessary and sometimes can't be done effectively, but it's a nice finishing touch when closing the loop comes naturally, as these two *Sports Illustrated* profiles demonstrate.

Here's the first paragraph of an *SI* piece by Steve Huffman and Rick Telander:

> My name is Steve Huffman. I'm 23 years old, 6'5", 270 pounds, and I'm a quitter.

And their last one-sentence graf:

> "The only thing I quit was Lou Holtz."

This lead is from an *SI* profile of Oakland A's slugger Jose Canseco by Rick Reilly:

Jose Canseco loves a good monster movie, with only one complaint. "Every time, the good guy wins," he says. "Why can't the monster ever win?"

Reilly's closing sentence:

Who says the monster never wins?

The first line of a *Business Week* article:

For decades, Walt Disney Co. has lived by this golden rule: Never underestimate the power of Mickey Mouse.

And the last line:

But don't tell the mouse.

The first sentence of a *New York Times* article:

Eli Finn eased his '78 Cadillac onto 1-95, heading for the history class he's taking at Fairfield University.

And the last:

By 2:10 he was back on 1-95. By 2:13 he was in the passing lane.

The lead paragraph from a *New York Times Magazine* profile:

Jodie Foster has only one regret. It came up one brutally hot day in August as she slouched in a warehouse in Cincinnati wearing a pair of blue gym shorts and a tank top. "The only thing I've ever regretted in my whole life," she said, stamping out a cigarette on the cement floor, "is that I started smoking."

And the closing sentence:

She is the good girl who knows that smoking cigarettes is bad.

Here's a two-paragraph lead from a Boise Cascade *Paper Times* feature:

Asked what was Oneco's chief claim to fame, Ken Marshall grinned and replied, "Well, it's next to Moosup, home of Walt Dropo." You remember Walt Dropo, nicknamed "Moose," the 6′5″ first baseman of the Boston Red Sox during the glory years of Ted Williams. In 1950 he hit 34 home runs, had 144 RBIs and a batting average of .322.

And the last paragraph:

Right next door to Walt Dropo.

So cinch the loop when you can. It's not vital, but it provides a nice finishing touch.

One last thing about features. When you think you're finally done, see if you haven't written a bit too much — a word, a sentence, a paragraph more than you should have. You'll be surprised how often you go just beyond your perfect ending.

CHAPTER 6

THE NEWS STORY:
STILL AN INVERTED PYRAMID

Not much has changed over the years in the construction of news stories. Journalism's *Who, What, When, Why, Where,* and *How* still make their joint appearance in the lead, usually in the first paragraph, certainly by the third. And because the straight news story's first obligation is to inform — to convey the pertinent facts quickly and clearly — the lead isn't a preamble to the story as it often is in a feature piece.

The lead is the story itself, skeletal yet intact for readers to flesh out if they care to continue reading. Or to dismiss and move on, content with the bare-bones information gleaned from the lead.

The news story's blueprint is still an upside-down pyramid, consisting of a summary lead tapering to the least-important details at the end, allowing editors to lop quickly from the bottom of the pyramid without damaging the structure.

News stories, being the workhorses they are, didn't used to have much personality, bred as they were for efficiency rather than showmanship — utility devoid of charm.

But not even newspapers are in the business of just disseminating news anymore. The mandate now is greater. Beyond an orderly presentation of the facts, stresses Jack Hart, writing coach of *The* (Portland) *Oregonian,* modem news writers have a few more obligations to their readers.

"It's true, our first public duty is a full and fair accounting of the day's news," acknowledges Hart, "and most of the stories we write take forms that serve that purpose."

But news writers should also recognize the ingredients of a good 'story' in the classic sense of the word. They should take the collection of abstract facts beyond the reach of a summary lead and an inverted pyramid of collective events. A newspaper links readers to the rest of humanity, Hart points out.

See Through Their Eyes

"It helps make life meaningful by exploring the nuances of the human condition. And by telling true stories in our paper, by relating human dramas that reveal central truths, we offer an added dimension to our readers. We help make life meaningful in a way no inverted-pyramid story can."

Good news writing — indeed, good writing of any kind — is essentially empathy, Hart sums up: "It's the ability to see things from the reader's viewpoint that determines whether a message gets through."

So reporters tend to launch their stories with softer leads these days to draw their readers in, help them put the facts into perspective, give them a glimpse of the larger meaning tucked into the progression of events that will follow. And readers are conceding writers more time to get to the heart of their stories, as this front-page *New York Times* piece demonstrates:

"What are those empty bottles on the floor?" the police officer asked the young man in a Yankees cap who sat behind the wheel. The motorist was pulled over in a random sobriety check late Friday on a dark highway outside this small farm town, about 45 miles west of Chicago. Police agencies around the country say motorists can expect to become much more familiar with such roadblocks after the United States Supreme Court ruled Thursday that they arc constitutional. Not long ago this story would have begun much more abruptly, perhaps with the bottom half of the second paragraph, minus all the introductory scene-setting: Police agencies around the country say motorists can expect to become much more familiar with sobriety roadblocks after the United States Supreme Court ruled them constitutional Thursday.

Another example of a soft news opening:

> Poor dad. He just wants to stretch out on a hammock and watch the clouds roll by. But no one will leave him alone. Not today. It is a day for loud tics, uneasy embraces and unmistakable colognes. Although the image and role of the father in American life has changed considerably in recent years, dad's day itself seems to resist updating.br>
> Father's Day is still more about barbecues and baseballs than flowers and fancy brunches. At special-occasion restaurants like the Russian Tea Room and Tavern on the Green, where Mother's Day is the busiest day of the year, it's just a normal Sunday, reservation managers say.

This writer took three paragraphs to let us in on the exact focus of his story: How Father's Day and Mother's Day differ in their celebration. Granted, it's light terrain the writer is treading, but it's the type of geography organizational communicators cover much of the time. However, if the category is "news" (defined loosely by *Webster's Collegiate Dictionary* as "a report of recent events") it's wise not to expect readers to delve too deeply into your copy for the gist of the matter at hand, conditioned as they are to getting the facts up front.

Mostly, therefore, news reporters must stand and deliver right up front, for that is their first order of business as evidenced by another *iNew York Tmes* front-page story on a fairly complicated subject. The piece went on to cover an additional 31 inches of newsprint, but the correspondent felt obligated to load his first three paragraphs with the salient facts and figures:

DALLAS, June 21 — In the mid-1980's the Stonebridge Ranch, a 6,250-acre development planned as a sprawling community of million-dollar homes, scenic golf courses and 13 man-made lakes, symbolized the vigor of the North Texas economy and the optimism of the aggressive savings and loan that poured an estimated $330 million into buying and upgrading the property. The Federal Government on Wednesday agreed to sell Stone-bridge Ranch, situated 30 miles north of Dallas, to a Japanese industrialist for $61 million. The savings and loan that once backed the development so eagerly was seized by the Government 18 months ago, after it was declared insolvent. The losses of nearly $270 million will be paid for by the American taxpayers. The sale is a striking example of the losses the Government is likely to face as it sells off the real estate it has seized from insolvent savings and loans — a crucial element in the Federal bailout of the industry.

A rule of thumb in presenting straight news without much redeeming personality is to begin the story as simply as possible and ease your readers into the complex details. In particular, don't cram unfamiliar names and meaningless titles into the lead, as was done in this *New York Times* lead:

The Treasury Department said today that Norman B. Ture, Under Secretary of the Treasury for Tax and Economic Affairs, did not profit from a Treasury contract for an economic forecasting model that Mr. Ture had developed and partly owned....After reviewing the matter the Justice Department has declined to prosecute, a Treasury Department spokesman said.

This cut-down version would have fed the facts sooner, mercifully allowing readers to move on:

After months of investigation, the Federal Government
has ruled out conflict-of-interest charges against an
under secretary who owned part of an economic
forecasting model bought by the Treasury Department.
The department found that he had made no profit.

Wire Services Dictated Style

Modern news stories are constructed much the same way they
have since the early 1900's when the wire services began
tailoring their copy to the demands of the teletype machine. "It
seemed almost as if the staccato movement of the machine had
been transmitted to the writing it produced," notes Philadelphia
journalism professor Waller Fox.

Sentences gradually shortened and turned overwhelmingly
to the active voice, Professor Fox pointed out. Excess adjectives
and adverbs were pruned to emphasize the verb. The lead took
on a life of its own, with painstaking effort devoted to its
construction. Wire service copy was tightly written and marked
by...the positioning of key words at the beginning of sentences
to heighten interest.

And the elements remain basically the same today:

A clear, concise summary lead, distilling the story's key
elements into a shot-glass slug of facts capable of standing alone
as a complete bulletin. The well-written lead flows cohesively
into succeeding paragraphs. Conversely, the poorly written lead
doesn't, a sure sign you'd better begin again.

A "secondary" lead that presents key facts and figures not
included in the summary lead. Not all stories, however, have a
secondary lead, necessary only when pertinent background
information is immediately important to the reader, despite its
interruption of the narrative flow.

An elaboration of the major elements of the story *in order of
diminishing interest*, hence the inverted pyramid structure. Think
in terms of herding the facts, quotes and data into a logical

sequence of information — cohesive segments in a descending hierarchy of importance.

All those components appear in this front-page story from a newsletter published for the pleasure-boat industry. First, the summary lead:

> Cahners Publishing, a major Boston-based trade and consumer publishing house, has agreed to buy *SAIL* magazine for an undisclosed price. The move follows the acquisition of *Power & Motoryacht* magazine by Cahners 18 months ago for a reported $40 million.

Then the secondary lead:

> The announcement that Cahners, part of Reed Publishing (USA) Inc., had signed a letter of intent with Meredith Corporation to buy *SAIL* was made in late May.

Followed by a paragraph-by-paragraph recitation of additional facts, figures and quotes in order of diminishing importance:

> Jeff Hammond, the 15-year magazine publishing veteran who founded *Power & Motoryacht* in 1984 and subsequently sold it to Cahners, will head up the Cahners Marine Publishing Group. Other magazines in the group include *MotorBoat* and *Motoryacht International.* Both Hammond and Donald Macaulay, publisher of *SAIL* said... John Beni, senior vice president and general manager of Cahners Consumer Division, described the acquisition as... Jack D. Rehm, president and CEO of Meredith, said...James A. Autry, president of Meredith's Magazine Group, said...

Trend Bucks Tradition

The momentum today is away from the traditional succession of "fractured" paragraphs — single units of thoughts linked by transitional words and phrases, as illustrated by this *New York Times* story on the glut of college graduates:

> Hundreds of thousands of jobs, once performed creditably without a college degree, are today going to college graduates as employers take advantage of an oversupply. College graduates are being found more and more among the nation's bakers, traveling salespeople, secretaries, bookkeepers, clerks, data processors and factory supervisors. And they are shutting out qualified high school graduates from many jobs, according to Labor Department officials, corporate executives and economists. Many jobs that were once relatively simple have grown complex, in large part because of new technologies. But the more important reason for the trend toward college graduates is that there are so many of them. At roughly 25 percent of the work force — higher than in any other industrial nation — college graduates outstrip the demand for their skills, the Labor Department reports. And the proportion of college graduates in the work force is continuing to increase.

Contrast *The New York Times' s* neatly packaged, orderly parade of facts above with *Newsweek's* everything-plus-the-kitchen-sink style of reporting, typified by this cover piece on flag burning. The first paragraph contains 162 words apportioned into seven sentences and a second paragraph that unravels 153 words in six sentences. I'll let you figure out how many separate ideas are shoehorned into these "suitcase" leads, as Roy Peter Clark calls them:

With the exception of veterans and schoolchildren, few Americans normally pause to observe Flag Day. But this year the nation's attention was riveted on Old Glory. Last week the Supreme Court struck down a federal flag-protection law, ruling 5 to 4 that although the desecration is offensive, it is a form of expression protected by the First Amendment. "Punishing desecration of the flag dilutes the very freedom that makes this emblem so revered, and worth revering," Justice William Brennan wrote for the majority. George Bush, who rode into office wrapped in the Stars and Stripes, immediately issued a call for a constitutional amendment banning desecration of the flag. As the GOP leadership jumped on the bandwagon — and Democrats played for time — amendment legislation began advancing through Congress. A House floor vote could come this week — the initial step in the campaign to alter the Bill of Rights for the first time in its 199-year history.

Take a deep breath and dive into the second paragraph:

However sincere people's feelings may be, the American flag also makes excellent politics. Flag-burning is a hot-button issue — a staple of the new *realpolitik*. "These issues are uniquely salient in a sound-bite era because they're visual and visceral," says Kathleen Jamison, dean of the communications school at the University of Pennsylvania. With the demise of communism throughout Eastern Europe, right-wing politicians in particular have struggled to fill the ideological vacuum with cultural 'values' issues. North Carolina Sen. Jesse Helms, who has led the continuing attack on the National Endowment for the Arts (NEA), has put obscenity on the conservative agenda and put it to good use in his direct-mail fund raising. The anti-porn movement moved into high relief last week when the Broward County, Fla., sheriff arrested two members of the Black rap band 2 Live Crew after a federal judge ruled one of their record albums obscene.

Whew!

To make sure this interminable piece wasn't a fluke, I leafed through more *Newsweek* issues. With one exception, every story I came across had leads plunging halfway to two-thirds down the first column, a style one newspaper writing coach refers to as "the big bloat."

Same Principles Apply

There's a vast difference, of course, in the importance of news stories found in daily newspapers and those usually encountered in company magazines and newsletters. Nonetheless, the same principles of editorial construction apply to both mediums, albeit in much briefer form in organizational publications.

To sum up again, the basic elements of a news story:

A concise summary lead of one or more paragraphs which encapsulate the story's key elements. A secondary lead immediately apprising readers of important background information left out of the summary lead. A detailed presentation of the story's major elements in the form of additional facts, quotes, and data, presented in order of diminishing interest. Hence, the inverted pyramid.

Students of business journalism need go no further than the pages of the *The Wall Street Journal* for a primer on how it ought to be done. Unabashed emulation of the *Journal's* distinctive style would not only constitute sincere flattery by corporate journalists, but also prove to be wise practice as well. Corporate wordsmiths prone to "elevating" the tone of their writing to pretentious levels should systematically dissect the diverting, down-to-earth style of this daily bible of the business community:

For more than 50 years, the five-pocket blue jeans made by Lee Cc of Merriam, Kan., were the uniform of cowboys and cowhands. Lee did a good, steady business, and that was enough to satisfy; the dry goods merchant Henry David Lee, who owned the company. But the once-stable jeans business has become extremely volatile and the Lee brand has fallen on hard times. Today it is trying for a comeback.

o

The way Oscar Wyatt figures it, war or no war, embargo or no embargo, Iraq has at least 100 billion barrels of crude oil in the ground So, throughout the Persian Gulf crisis, the controversial Texas oil man has made sure Iraq knows he's a friend. Before Saddam Hussein invaded Kuwait, Mr. Wyatt's company was one of the world's biggest buyers of Iraqi crude. Now that there's peace, he wants at that oil again.

o

The homeless, long a big-city phenomenon, arc emerging as a rural crisis, too. Ask Lowell Rott. After his small, debt-ridden farm hen was auctioned off on the courthouse steps in 1986, he slept for a time in his 1973 Dodge pickup. Now he's a squatter in an abandoned two room house with no running water. There isn't much demand for 50-year-old farmers like him. A high school dropout, he works as a handyman for $10 a day and shower privileges. The faded old suit he wears for job interviews it town hasn't made him more attractive. His face is streaked with cinders from a wood stove that generates so little heat he wears a parka to bed. He stubbornly keeps a hand in farming by raising castoff horses on the land of sympathetic neighbors. "The horses are homeless and so am I," he says. "We belong together."

o

Good night, Vietnam. The lightning-quick victory in the Persian Gulf War did more than sweep Iraq out of Kuwait. It is sweeping the Vietnam War from the forefront of the American consciousness.

A lead from *Forbes:*

DEAR HERB: Congratulations on a magnificent coup with your investment in Steve Ross' Warner Communications! But what are you doing for an encore? When Ross convinced the corporate bureaucrats at Time Inc. to pay $70 a share in cash and securities to Warner in 1989, the Warner shares held by your BHC Communications Inc. became worth $2.4 billion — five times what you paid for the stock less than six years earlier.

The lead of a *Fortune* cover story:

Oh, those foolish optimists! Had anyone said three months ago that the 28-nation coalition would steamroller Saddam, that Wall Street's bull would be roaring, interest rates still falling, and the economy showing signs of recovery — that person would have been laughed out of the bar. Yet the optimists (and George Bush, Dick Cheney, and Colin Powell) have been proved right.

Two leads from *Business Week:*

Robert Maxwell pursues Rupert Murdoch the way racehorses used to chase Secretariat: from several lengths back. So it seems apt that the British media baron is now challenging his rival's primacy at the track.

o

Perhaps you've heard it on a late-night cross-country light. Or on a commuter train. Or maybe in the waiting room at your doctor's office. At any time of day or night, and just about anywhere, you can trace that click-click-clicking — to an executive, a salesperson, or a student hunched over the keyboard of a tiny laptop computer.

Lacking Personality

Now contrast the confident, unselfconscious exuberance of the copy above with the demureness displayed in the organizational news stories below. Though competently constructed and tightly written, they beg vigor and emotion, often viewed as unbecoming traits in corporate journalism:

With the price of software kraft pulp nearly doubling in the past three years, major pulp producers currently have more than 50 new expansion projects underway worldwide.

o

Your fitness and good health will be the subject of a 12-month series of presentations offered by the Human Resources and Education and Training Departments, in cooperation with Health Advancement Services, Camelback Hospitals' speakers' bureau and local nonprofit organizations.

o

After a two-year lull, recruiters from ARCO Oil and Gas Co.'s facility in Piano, Texas, went hunting for talent again last fall. And they found slim pickings — stiff competition within the industry for a shrinking pool of both young and experienced engineers and geoscientists.

o

The Residential and Building Controls Divisions at Golden Valley have announced a major office paper recycling program.

o

To kick off its program on June 15, each employee was given a black spruce or Scotch pine tree seedling. "Not only does a paper recycling program conserve our valuable resources but it also significantly reduces landfill space requirements," said Barbara Hensley, manager of customer service.

Tips on Quoting

Given the fact that news stories usually blend a fairly even mix of facts interspersed with quotes, get into the habit of introducing the person you're quoting as early as possible. The first natural pause in the initial sentence is a good place, especially if that first sentence is a long one. In the paragraph above, the speaker could have been identified sooner than she was ("Not only does a paper recycling program conserve our valuable resources," said Barbara Hensley, manager of customer service, "but...").

Not only is it good form to let the reader in on who's doing the talking at the earliest opportunity, but the technique also makes your writing more crisp. See if the second sentence below doesn't pick up the reading tempo just a bit:

"Yeah, some of the equipment is old," says Dale Anderson, sawmill supervisor.

"Yeah," says sawmill supervisor Dale Anderson, "some of the equipment is old."

A few words on stretching too hard for synonyms to replace the attributive verb "says" or "said": Don't! Save your creativity for where it's needed. The old workhorse does a good-enough job of linking speakers with their words, and readers are oblivious to its endless repetition. Reaching for imaginative descriptions such as "asserted." "demanded," "suggested," "quipped," "questioned," "exclaimed," or "maintained" in straight news stories merely strains credibility. It isn't worth the effort or the cost.

Another good reason for introducing your speaker a few words into the quote instead of after the initial set of quotation marks is that you end the sentence with a more evocative word than the person's name or title. Take this paragraph from a *Weyerhaeuser Today* story:

> "I figured they'd probably say 'get out of here, we're busy' — but I thought it was worth a try," adds Sermonti.

The sentence closes with Sermonti's name, which the readers already know. Injecting the speaker into the quote sooner ends the line with a lean word that catapults the reader into the next paragraph:

> "I figured they'd probably say 'get out of here, we're busy,' " adds Sermonti, "but I thought it was worth a try."

A sound rule, whether you're writing news stories or features, is to bound from one sentence to the next, and into each succeeding paragraph, gathering momentum as you go. Use every trick you know to keep your readers moving forward, ever onward, to the end of your story.

"One of journalism's worst legacies is the lack of attention to endings," bemoans Jack Hart, a former managing editor with *The Oregonian* and the Portland newspaper's writing coach for many years: "It's probably the result of the inverted pyramid story that allows editors to start cutting at the bottom and trim away all but the first graf without losing the story's central point."

That's fine, Hart concedes, but he reminds us of William Zinsser's sage advice that writers should give as much thought to their last sentence as to their first — well, almost as much.

"The ending is a story's crowning touch," says Hart. "It's the last taste, what readers carry away from the newspaper, the bit they remember best because it's freshest in their minds. The well-crafted finish gives a sense of completion, a wrapping up that leaves readers feeling satisfied."

To illustrate, Hart provides a few happy endings from past pages of his own newspaper.

A story on a sand castle-building contest began this way: "In the beginning, there was mud." And ended:

> Finally, as the crowd retreated, the Pacific lapped at the creations, reclaiming the sand to re-create the familiar beach. Ashes to ashes, mud to mud.

This was the melodious wrap of a day-in-the-life look at a fitness resort:

> As darkness closes in around the picturesque villas tucked among the hills, the mood is tranquil, the air cool. A few figures walk briskly around the track that circles a grove of fruit trees. The only sound is the thump of a tennis ball in the distance. For the moment, routine concerns have been forgotten. The mind seems clear. The body feels restored.

And a wonderful ending that had to be the story's most memorable line:

> "I love working with kids," he said. "They still don't know how to hate."

"Don't let your story fade out like an overgrown path disappearing into the woods," counsels Hart.

"The ending colors the reader's perception of everything that came before. It's critical enough to the whole piece to spend some extra time and effort looking for the perfect close to a story that deserves the best possible send-off."

CHAPTER 7

THE VITAL ART OF INTERVIEWING

Sources. They are the all-important people who possess the information you need for your writing. Interviews are your primary means of securing that information. And how skillfully you accomplish this deft extraction determines the ultimate quality of your copy.

Never minimize the importance of the delicate art of interviewing. Or haphazardly prepare for its crucial undertaking.

"No matter how fine a writer might be," says *Writer's Digest* editor John Brady, "he is crippled if he is not an effective interviewer. Today's reader wants more than bare facts," adds Brady. "He wants to know why an event occurred, what feelings it incited, how it might have been avoided."

Exacting editors, says Brady, demand that their journalists know more than just the card tricks of writing. They must know how to probe their sources for "the telling detail, the taut quote."

To aid you in your vital pursuit of the pithy remark, the spirited rejoinder, the pregnant pause, and the cogent comment, here are some tips on sharpening that most powerful of communication tools: the interview.

Relax. Don't make it more complicated than it is. As important as it is to your final product, basically an interview is no more than a chat, a casual get-together to secure some information and a few quotes. Stress the offhandedness of the occasion. In fact, avoid the word "interview" altogether. It implies a formal — to some, even a confrontational encounter.

Say instead, "I'd like to get your thoughts on a few things." And always specify the amount of time you'll require. If the session goes well, the interviewee probably will volunteer the extra time you'll need. Or you can suggest a follow-up meeting or a phone call to fill in the blank spots.

Explain what you're after. When setting up the initial interviews, take a few minutes to go over the ground you'll be covering and how you'll be using the information you seek. Make it clear exactly what you're after in the way of details, information, explanations, or instructions.

Let interviewees know if you'll be getting into some sensitive areas. And assure them if you won't. Fully apprising interviewees beforehand will give them time to collect their thoughts, which should make the sessions more productive.

Especially encourage the people you interview to recall any pertinent anecdotes and stories. Remember, they are the heart and soul of lively, readable articles. A good way to prime the pump for such material is to recite one or two anecdotes from your research on the subjects to be covered.

Urge interviewees to jot down some thoughts and feelings beforehand. "Picture yourself reading the article when it's in print," you might suggest, "and chastising yourself for not saying exactly what you wanted. Well, here's your chance to think about what you'd like to say."

The resulting quotes may not be spontaneous, but they'll be thought out. There'll be time enough during the interview to try for spontaneity. First, strive for relevance and accuracy.

On the subject of accuracy, a mandatory follow-up question is: "How do you *know* this?" Ask it often.

Come prepared. Do your homework beforehand — on the person and the subject. Then show by your questions and remarks that you've come well-prepared. It will pay off in dividends. Besides, it's inexcusable for a writer — and disrespectful — for a writer not to be thoroughly prepared (and appropriately dressed) for the interview.

Prepare a list of questions — more than you'll need. Even if you plan not to use all of them, scanning them occasionally will ensure you touch all the conversational bases you had planned to cover.

"Let's just talk" is the sort of casual tone you want to set, even though you're dead-serious about coming away with everything you need for your story. In an atmosphere of casualness, you'll get better material.

Make some of your questions personal and interesting — fun to answer. If you know the person has an avid pastime, try to ask him about it: how he got into the hobby, why he enjoys it. Don't make the interview drudgery; if you do, it will show in the replies, the all-important quotes you depart with.

Ask a few questions to which you already know the answers, suggests Bruce Henderson. "If the source tells me something different," reasons the veteran freelance writer, "I know he's either lying or misinformed. Whichever the case, not passing those test-questions will impugn the rest of what he tells me."

Author Cornelius Ryan carried it a step further. Never interview anyone, he counseled, without knowing at least 60 percent of the answers.

Ease In

Break the ice. Don't charge right into the business at hand. Begin with a pleasantry or two, a compliment if it comes naturally, or an ingratiating remark. Put the person — and yourself — at ease. Try to establish some rapport. The best interviews come in a conversational setting of kinship and trust. But don't get familiar or smart-alecky. Behave like the guest that you are.

Ask permission before using a recording device. And turn it off if or when you're asked. Start with the soft stuff. Lob in a few, then signal that you're ready for hardball with a solid, well-thought-out question. It *will* make an impression.

During the interview, if you sense the going is getting sluggish, suggest a break. Ask interviewees if there's a phone call they may need to make. Ask for a glass of water. Compliment the person on his or her progress if it's warranted — or even if it's not. Say the interviewee is working hard and that you're getting some good stuff.

Park your ego. Remember why you're there. Let the other person be the star and do all the talking. Inject yourself only when you have to, not merely to show off your erudition or wit. Try to keep the interviewee's comments coming. And the best way to do that is to listen hard. Evidence your interest through eye-contact and body language.

Listen "empty" as Stuart Kamen puts it. Picture your mind as a glass or bucket waiting to be filled. Don't assume you know what's going to be said because anything new or unexpected will just overflow the crowded receptacle. Keep your consciousness and notebook poised and ready.

Lean forward, nod, shake your head, laugh, smile, frown, ask for clarification once in a while or for more details. Offer an occasional "Uh-huh," "I see," even an enthusiastic "Wow, that is so true!" if the response is warranted to evidence your attention and keep the conversation moving briskly. Your obvious interest could mean the difference between a lively, free-flowing dialogue and a dull, self-conscious monologue..

Show enthusiasm for what you're hearing if that's what you feel it, but don't show disapproval or criticism except to spark a deliberate, calculated response. A good technique, if you have the self-assurance to carry it off, is to treat famous people as if they weren't particularly special (even idolatry gets tiresome) and "ordinary" people as if they were quite special indeed. Again, though, common respect is always mandatory, regardless whom you're interviewing.

Try the silent treatment. A wonderful interview technique is to ask a tough or critical question, then let the person's answer hang in mid-air — as if you were expecting more. Silence can be golden at times like this because it begs to be broken. And when you let the interviewee do it, chances are you'll wind up with some great quotes you wouldn't have gotten if you'd plunged into your next question.

Another effective technique, particularly toward the end of the interview, is to put your pen away or turn off the tape recorder. The person may keep talking — much less guardedly — giving you the best lines of the day.

Watch the time. Impress on the interviewee with solicitous remarks and an occasional glance at your watch that you're indeed aware of the time you've been granted — and grateful for it.

Try to end the interview when you should. If the session's going well and there's still information to relay, the interviewee may insist you stay or suggest another meeting. Just don't take his or her time for granted.

"A lot of interviews run long," counsels Maryland freelancer Carolyn Mulford, "and often the key part will be near the end. Leave a cushion of time before your next appointment so you don't have to dash away or make a call just when you're getting to the meat of the matter."

Debrief yourself. As soon as possible after the interview, go back over your notes. Make sure they're legible to you. Embellish them if necessary while your memory still serves. Enter additional notations. Flesh out key thoughts, observations, and feelings. Debrief yourself fully on paper while everything is still fresh in your mind.

Fine-tune quotes. If the recorded comments you come away with aren't that great, consider "fixing" them — within the bounds of journalistic propriety, of course. Don't change the meaning of the quoted material, just tighten the words. Give them a bit more impact or cohesion — again, without altering their meaning.

Consolidate the person's thoughts, rephrasing the remarks for clarity if necessary. Just make sure you review changes with interviewees before attributing the words to them in print. Few people object to being made eloquent and witty. Or less pedantic and dull. Remember, you're not a court reporter. Everything you're told doesn't have to be related verbatim.

The objective isn't to provide readers with a faithful transcription of what was said, but to convey the ideas succinctly and readably. So keep the quotes natural. Don't turn conversation into corporatese. If what's said to you is, indeed, corporatese, don't put it into quotes in your written piece. Paraphrase the information instead.

The New York Times quoted one source in this fashion, no doubt because it was exactly what the man said: "I am currently designing a line of mirrored Venetian furniture with an eighteenth-century look that will also go here, too." The sentence would have been better had "also" or "too" been deleted. In this case, total accuracy served no purpose other than to detract from the quote.

Beware, too, of "inventory journalism." Don't use a quote from every interview you conduct just to prove you talked to a bunch of people.

Give Star Billing

When you get a great quote, put it up in lights. *The New York Times* got so carried away with a spectacular quote, it did just that — ran a quote that had no right in the secondary lead of a front-page story detailing an Irish Republican Army assault on London's 10 Downing Street. But the remark was so exquisitely British, it received star billing nevertheless:

> London, Feb. 7 — Three mortar rounds were fired from a van this morning toward the offices of Prime Minister John Major in 10 Downing Street, scoring a hit in the backyard as he presided over his war Cabinet. The Irish Republican Army later took responsibility for the attack, in which three people were slightly wounded. "I think we'd better start again somewhere else," a startled Mr. Major told the group as a loud bang cracked but did not shatter the bulletproof windows in the Cabinet room. There was no structural damage to the building, which is also the Prime Minister's official residence, and none of the country's top military and civilian officials were hurt. Mr. Major and the Cabinet then moved their meeting to a room in an adjoining building.

Much more critical to the context of the story, though less entertaining than the prime minister's imperturbable reaction to the terrorist attack, was another quote that comprised the fourth paragraph of the story. In terms of relative importance, it should have been the secondary lead:

> "I think it is clear that it was a deliberate attempt this morning both to kill the Cabinet and to do damage to our democratic system of government," Mr. Major told the House of Commons this afternoon.

So even *The New York Times* can be seduced by alluring quotes.

Comments such as Mr. Major's above are editorial gems, indeed, well worth the excavation, for they imbue organizational writing with much-needed vitality.

What's more, earthy, eloquent quotes impart instant credibility because they are not only attention-grabbing but ring instantly true, bestowing immediacy and credibility.

Great quotes can't be fabricated. They either happen or they don't, and when they do they are unquestionably real. When they are made up, they are patently false.

Other examples of clearly authentic quotes:

> Paul Schuback is asked how he knows merely by scrutinizing the wood that it's right for the cello he is creating. "I *know*," replies the master maker. "When you put broccoli in your mouth, you can tell it isn't cauliflower."

o

> "Blindness is a nuisance," said Joyce Castle, who is 23 years old and blind. "But it's not the greatest handicap."

o

The woman sat on a stool and ordered the waiter to remove all the salt and pepper shakers from the counter. Then she warned him, "Don't try to bring any of that jam out either."

o

"Politics isn't his thing," says a confidant. "It's like a fancy suit. He can imagine trying it on, but it just doesn't fit."

o

"He was a pussycat after his heart attack. Before that, I dreaded working with him. Look in Lewis's mouth. He's got three rows of teeth."

o

"This was *a* bungled job from start to finish," Des Moines's police Sgt. Mitch Barker said. "All we needed was Curly. We had Larry and Moe."

o

"Everywhere I belong," says the Eurasian author of *Slow Burn*, who grew up in Australia and Manila, "and everywhere I'm an outsider."

To a writer, such quotes are like found money. When they happen to you, you'll want to share them with your readers as soon as possible. Leading off an article with a quote, some say, is amateurish, but the great ones usually land right up front, where they belong.

CHAPTER 8

WRITER'S BLOCK, JUMP STARTS, CREATIVITY

"Why haven't you finished our distress marker?" Hagar the Horrible asks Lucky Eddy in the popular comic strip drawn by cartoonist Dik Brown.

"I have writer's block," replies a distraught Eddie as Hagar glowers at the two letters spelled out in rocks on the sand: "S. 0."

Writer's constipation! Like Lucky Eddy, most of us are stricken with it regularly. It's the wordsmith's common affliction, the chronic malady of our profession. Except that suffering from it once doesn't make anyone immune. Far from it.

What can you do about writer's block when it rears its languid head?

I had one of those days only last week, good only for such mindless diversions as flipping through my Gary Larson desktop calendar. I began flipping through the pages midway in June and was almost through November before forcing myself to stop.

Before I finally did, however, I came across a "Far Side" cartoon that provided me a bit of solace. It depicted a man clutching his head in frustration over a table piled with crumpled sheets of paper on which were scribbled "Call me Al." "Call me Bill." "Call me Roger." "Call me Warren."

Poor Herman. When he settled on "Ishmael" I trust the rest of his novel took off like the Pequot chasing old Moby. So even the immortal Melville fought writer's block, according to Larson.

Every Writer's Nemesis

Writers will go to any lengths to dislodge this dark usurper of their precious productivity and unclog their creative pipes.

Success lies in a positive mental attitude, claims Lawrence Block. Believe in yourself and your ability to the point of wiping out all negative thoughts, suggests the *Writer's Digest* columnist. Replace them with "affirmations" (positive, can-do feelings). Then move on. And don't look back.

The process *will* succeed, promises Block: "Anyone who works effectively with affirmations will be less at the mercy of implanted negative thoughts and will consequently write more lucidly. The first step in getting your own way is getting out of your own way, and affirmations are as good a means toward that end as I know."

Sounds like a plan, though a long-term one at the minimum, even a lifetime proposition.

Unfortunately, our American way is the quick fix, an instant remedy, a magic formula in a flip-top can that whisks away all mental, physical, and emotional impediments to our creative expression with a gentle gurgle and grateful hiss. We're all looking for the Alka Seltzer of our professional blockage.

My own instant relief came in the form of three little words that banished writer's block forever: *Lower your standards.* To which I tacked on a second directive: *Temporarily.* And capped the four words with a third mandate: *Now get started.*

Nothing had helped my mental constipation until I came across this magnificent laxative. A workshop lecturer uncorked it for me several years ago. I've since forgotten exactly when and where — even the man's name and what he was talking about, but his nugget of advice will glisten in my memory forever.

How often do we not start something simply because we're afraid of failing? Well, no problem. If you can't raise your confidence level, then lower the goal. Just for a while. Then get on with it.

Fast Starts

Another way to overcome writer's block is to get a jump on your work every morning. Blast off. Get yourself moving with as little waste-motion as possible. Outdistance the blahs before they close in on you. There are as many ways to jump-start yourself as there are remedies for writer's block. Some aren't bad, must don't work, but a few actually do. For sure, they're all worth a try.

A freelance writer I know gets up at five every weekday morning, not to read or write or exercise, but to quietly sip three successive cups of coffee in the gathering light of the new day. In this reflective time, he allows whatever thoughts, ideas, feelings, fears, inspiration, or creativity lurking out there to seep into his consciousness.

"I sometimes wind up scribbling snatches of copy," he says, "but mostly I just sit in the dark letting my mind drift. Or I mentally pick my way through a problem. Or I energize myself for the moment I sit down at the keyboard. That first hour is the most important of each working day," he reveals. "It sets the tone, the mood, paves the way for everything to follow."

Another writer I know spends an hour on her exercise bike with a notepad and pencil dangling from its handlebars to capture any thoughts that come her way. "They always do," she says. "The sweat and adrenaline seem to stoke my creative energy."

A freelancer told me he goes for early morning runs, letting his thoughts and ideas float in and out of his head with the rhythm of his strides. It's how he gets mentally and emotionally ready to write. "I prepare the same way you paint a house," he said. "You don't just start splashing paint. First there's the mental furniture to be moved out of the way and drop cloths and masking tape to be put down. Many writers just jump in and start spraying latex. For me, it's not only sloppy but ineffective. I don't start until I'm ready, until I've exercised the words consciously and subconsciously while I'm running."

Yet there are writing instructors who advise sitting down and "just writing." Getting the thoughts down on paper, then going back and rearranging them later. The trouble, too often, is that a writer's impulsive stream of expression comprises a vortex of words that spin him around and around until he realizes a simple, frustrating fact — he doesn't know what he's trying to say.

When you know what you're trying to say, the words come easily. When you don't, they come hard, or don't make much sense when they do.

So maybe it takes moving the mental furniture first, arranging the drop cloths before painting the creative images.

Cooking Up Steam

One of the best ways I know to get up a head of steam each morning is to make sure you don't have something new to start — an article, issue, project, whatever. Writers soon figure out that getting going is half the battle. And some make it as easy as possible to get themselves moving by using momentum left over from the day before.

Their advice is not to finish a piece of writing before you quit each evening. Leave the article, the chapter, the page, the paragraph, even the sentence hanging there for you to grab onto in the morning. A great place to stop, for instance, is in the midst of transcribing a quote, or editing an article, or reworking a first draft-anything that helps you get off to a rolling start. If you can't pick up the next day in the middle of something, another way to get going is to retype a paragraph or two, even a whole page if that's what it takes to build up some momentum.

Or jump to another section of the piece to get yourself unstuck. Start writing a part that gets your juices flowing.

Or edit what you've already written — but not all of it, for the objective is to get moving. Go back a page or two, just enough to warm up.

Reward Yourself

Some writers dangle incentives and rewards for getting into a piece. A coffee-lover deprives herself of that first exquisite cup until she's met her quota of a page or two. A crossword addict treats himself to a puzzle — *after* he's earned it.

Just don't put the carrot, the latte, the puzzle, the chapter from the novel you're reading *ahead* of the work.

The toughest part is getting started. Figure out how to do that, and you'll have it made. But if you can't get going no matter what, throw in the towel — just for a while. Do some other work, even if it's not writing.

Take research material into the park to read. Make a few phone calls. Tackle those phone interviews you were going to postpone for another day. Or have an early lunch. Go for a walk, ride your bike, walk the dog. Get away, clear your mind, then come back and try again.

The only question to ask yourself: What works for *me*?

"Any discipline or indulgence that actually helps nudge you into position facing the page is acceptable and productive," say novelist-writing instructor Janet Burroway. "If jogging after breakfast energizes your mind, then jog before you sit. If you have to pull an all-nighter on a coffee binge, do that. If you have to be chained to your chair, invest in a chain. And if, like me, you are one of the unlucky ones driven by guilt, then welcome your guilt and make sure it drives you toward the desk rather than away."

Need a motto? Burroway suggests her own, the one hanging above her desk: "Don't Dread. Do."

On Becoming More Creative

Moving to the opposite end of the spectrum, let's explore a talent that's fascinated humankind through the centuries, because the people blessed with it are the trailblazers of history.

The rest of us merely tuck into their wakes, feeding on their originality, and embellishing their breakthroughs.

Creativity. Everyone covets it. Psychologists are studying it, hoping that if they can dissect originality, they can duplicate it. A study of 200 college students showed that creative people fall asleep faster than non-creative types and hatch their solutions while dreaming.

So even corporate types, long fixated solely on proven effectiveness and assured accuracy are open to right-brain solutions. By all means, strive to be creative in all your communications presentations, but not *too* creative, for most business people don't trust innovation, many fear it, and some wouldn't recognize it if it stood up and mooned them.

Make no mistake, creativity is universally desirable, but only if it's tried and true, rendered familiar and comfortable like old slippers by repeated usage.

Creativity, certainly, should be the hallmark of the organizational communicator's endeavors, which is why I research the subject periodically in the hope that some of what I discover will rub off on me. Here's some of what I've pondered on the intriguing subject.

Booze doesn't nurture or enhance creativity. It only seems to, reports British psychologist Geoff Lowe, who clinically tested the age-old theory that alcohol and imaginative thinking go glass-in-hand. Lowe assembled 32 moderate drinkers aged 18 to 30 for two testing periods spaced a week apart. At the first session, each member of the group drank a glass of water and tonic. Lowe then administered a standard creativity test. At the second session, each drank a glass of vodka and tonic before taking the test.

He discovered that members of the group who had scored low on the test after a water and tonic responded more creatively with a shot or two of alcohol. But those who'd scored high when sober saw things much less creatively when moderately drunk.

Lowe's conclusion was that alcohol tends to shed inhibitions in less-creative people but has the opposite effect on more-creative individuals. The latter, he says, are already operating at an optimum level, and the booze merely harms their performance. Besides, liquor really does kill brain cells.

So much for drinking on the job.

Hypnosis can grease the flow. Since the creation process basically involves focusing inward, points out New York psychotherapist Berty Kronsky, self-hypnosis, biofeedback, and other self-centering rituals can help free and inspire the mind. A plethora of such self-help primers can be found in today's on-line and dead-tree bookstores.

It's OK to let creativity scare you. Condition your managers to accept that originality isn't supposed to be like a favorite pair of slippers, instantly comfortable. If your supposedly creative copy feels "right" to you from the start, if the flow of it comes too easily, look at what you've written again — hard. Original thoughts, by their very uniqueness, are unfamiliar, disconcerting, and even scary. Some of the best ideas seem illogical, even idiotic in the beginning. Give them time.

Failing is worth the risk. Nothing is more destructive to creativity than fear of failure. If you're not willing to fail, don't try to be creative. Put your energy instead into emulating some of what's already succeeded. Copy the examples. No shame in that.

Be receptive to ideas. Your own and those of others, regardless of how half-baked, far-fetched, or downright silly they seem. The more open you are to new thoughts, attitudes, experiences, and other professionals, the greater your chances of being truly creative.

Take notes — a lot of them. The creative process, said radio/TV comedian-author Steve Allen, is enhanced when you give the brain as much relevant raw material as possible.

Be humble. Pride impedes the search [or wisdom and originality, adds Allen, so develop the old-fashioned virtue of humility as you explore new interests, situations, and people. Being humble will open you up to fresh thoughts and creative solutions. Pride will block them.

Maximize right-brain, minimize left-brain activities. Decide what you are, what you want to be — a right-brainer or a left-brainer — and act accordingly. It's hard to be outstanding at both. And one set of activities usually detracts from the other.

Impose as few "rules" as possible. On yourself. On others. Freedom is the mulch that nurtures creativity. Frequent evaluation inhibits it. Constant, carping criticism throttles it. Hands-off management is the ticket here. Simply leave good people alone, in the view of Massachusetts Institute of Technology Nobel laureate Dr. Salvador Luria, and they'll do fine.

Unfortunately, Luria's advice goes hugely and directly against the grain of most business managers, who have been taught all these years: control, control, control! How do you tell a manager not to manage so much anymore? I don't know. But I'll think about it while I give Dr. Luria another round of cheers.

Go state-of-the-art. The latest technology, both hard and soft, is a quantum asset to you as an organizational writer-editor, in terms of creativity as well as productivity. *Must* reading, therefore, are William Zinsser's *Writing with a Word Processor* and Jeremy Hewes' *Writing in the Computer Age.*

Encourage "abnormalcy." What kills creativity? Normalcy, claims advertising notable Edward McCabe, in an address to an industry group:

> Any semblance of creativity not drummed out of us at school, society at large will beat out of us. We are taught that to belong, we must dress in a certain manner, cultivate certain friends, drive certain cars, live in particular neighborhoods, drink certain drinks. Upon entering our chosen professions, the anti-creative training continues, pointing us toward certain restaurants, clubs and so on. Belonging is the ultimate goal. Anyone failing to do so becomes a social outcast. In youth they're called delinquents. Later on in life they're referred to as troublemakers and rabble-rousers. If, by some miracle, against incredible odds, they

manage to go their own ways and, even more incredible, succeed at it, well, then they're often called something else: Genius.

McCabe's point: "Everyone is conditioned from an early age toward normality, whatever that is. What it isn't is creative."

Resist regimentation in every way. A NEAT DESK IS THE SIGN OF A DERANGED MIND. The first time I saw those words stenciled on a paperweight in an office I'll charitably describe as "lived in," my heart leaped in exultation. Like the older President Bush and other adults who hate broccoli because they were forced to eat it as children, I delight in particularly messy work-areas, mine as well as everyone else's — because for years I was forced to keep an extremely neat one.

Not at Creativity's Expense

I once had a boss who regarded everyone who worked for him, along with the furniture, wall art, and office decor in his department as his personal property and direct reflection of his management style. One of his passions was an orderly desk during the working day — and a spotless one at night, which meant that literally everything on each desk had to be swept into the drawers before the staff departed the premises each night.

The rationale for this tyrannical neatness was that the cleaning crew couldn't dust properly if debris cluttered the desktops. Secretly, though, I think the manager reveled in the knowledge that if the chief executive officer ever mounted a pre-dawn inspection of the premises, his communications department would be — well, *neat* — *i*ts uncluttered desks gleaming like so many polished skulls aligned in neat rows.

Secure in that rationale, he never imagined how dearly his compulsive tidiness cost his writers and editors.

The New York consulting firm of Booz Allen Hamilton once published a report revealing that the efficient organization of executive work space can boost productivity by 15 percent.

And probably cut creativity in half, for there is something about the creative mind and heart that recoils from complete orderliness, from a regimentation of appearance and routine.

Keep in mind, too, that writing productivity cannot be standardized either. All writers have their own way of working, and each one's method should be respected. Pulitzer Prize-winning sports writer Red Smith never wrote a second draft. But he'd tear up leads and throw them away by the bushel basket until he got exactly the right one-then he proceeded from there. Can you picture a time-study consultant advising Mr. Smith on how to shore up this aspect of his productivity?

Acknowledging that business environments must have certain operational parameters, nonetheless, heads of communication departments with so-called "creative" individuals should be prepared to accept the different drumbeats of their marchers. Within reason, of course.

Certainly organizational writers and editors should be allowed to create working environments conducive to their optimum creativity. Including unkempt desks, if that's what it takes.

CHAPTER 9

DEFINING, TAILORING YOUR PUBLICATION

Most successful organizational publications are the extension of one person's talent and skills: The editor's. That individual, therefore, should be given the freedom and control to create the communications vehicle in his or her image, consistent, of course, with the organization's mission and goals. Only then can it hope to achieve some character and charisma — a personality of its own.

Acknowledging up front that corporate magazines and newsletters are, first and foremost, management tools with specific aims and necessary restrictions, they can and should possess more than a modicum of flair, vitality, and charisma if they are to communicate. They must reflect the humanity of the individuals who shepherd each issue from creative concept to printed or on-line reality in that both writer and reader are flesh-and-blood composites of the interests, appetites, ambitions, and desires that drive us all.

Believe this, therefore: There is no such thing as a "captive" audience, even though the organizational communicator comes as close to owning one as any editor ever will. Still, you can't count on anyone reading what you write simply because he or she happens to work for your company. Or because they are members of your association or agency or office or church. Or because what you've written may affect their jobs or could make them smarter, eventually richer employees, and even better human beings.

Those self-serving motivations aren't good enough because most of us don't have the time or inclination to digest anything else — we have so much on our plates already — no matter what mental, physical, or emotional rewards we might accrue.

115

Perhaps the reluctance dates back to our earliest school days when we were doled increasingly larger reading assignments. Now that we don't have teachers compelling us to read, our attention must be earned — a formidable task in this age of intense competition for our fleeting interest. You can count, therefore, on people reading what you write for one reason only — because they can't help themselves.

Only Two Kinds of Writing

What's more, in our business there are only two kinds of writing — good and bad. Good writing gets read, bad writing doesn't. So nothing written is worth the paper or computer screen on which it appears unless it is interesting, informative, or entertaining enough to snare our elusive attention.

"That's certainly the way it is with organizational and business magazines," affirms *Dallas* magazine editor Sheri Rosen.

"No one really has time to read them, not thoroughly or regularly," says Rosen. "But, for whatever reasons, our readers still want publications — if only to maintain a sense of connection with the company — or to scan while they're watching a dull television show, or to take home so the kids can cut out the photographs for school projects."

Classroom cut-ups notwithstanding, your main objective is to get your newsletter read. Isn't that the only reason for publishing or posting *any* words? In the real world of organizational communicators, the answer would be a cynical no, the main goal of organizational writers is to catapult themselves into management.

It's why the International Council of Industrial Editors (ICIE) changed its name a number of years ago to the International Association of Business Communicators (IABC). Because organizational writing and editing jobs, for the most part, remain entry-level ramps on the corporate road to bigger and better things.

I'd like to show you how to propel yourself from a stack of exemplary newsletters to the giddy heights of corporate success without honing your writing and editing skills. I'd like to open a bag of tricks, slip you some pills, chart a few shortcuts to painless success.

I'd like to, but I can't.

This book, as its title suggests, is mostly about writing: How to produce readable communication pieces by becoming a skilled, creative writer and editor. Your own ambition will have to propel you the rest of the way, whatever your destination.

I can assure you, though, that the effort you put into your writing *will* pay off over the course of your career, for the ability to communicate lucidly, forcefully, persuasively, is at the heart of sound management.

First, Understanding

First on the path to effective organizational writing and editing looms the task of clearly understanding and defining both your audience and how you intend to motivate it. This brings us to editorial planning-a chore you'd rather avoid, I'm sure, if you're like most right-brained people. But it's important in this business because it saves time, aggravation, and company money. It makes both you and your publication more effective. It simplifies the creation of each issue and reduces wasted effort. And it makes your work more enjoyable. It could even mean your leaving the office on time — occasionally anyway.

To develop a plan that looks at an entire year rather than the contents of a single issue at a time, you must determine the editorial objectives of your publication, and then decide how much space should be allocated to each end. This is left-brain stuff. The creative part comes in deciding *how* to achieve those objectives with your editorial content. And then doing it.

Start by coming up with some honest answers to a few questions:

- Do I really know my readers? Or do I seldom consider them? Am I really producing the publication for my boss and a few peers?
- Do I see my readers as flesh-and-blood people?
- Do I empathize with them, understand their daily concerns?
- How much of what I'm trying to force-feed them do they already know? Do they care? What do they *need* to know?
- Is my publication in its current format the best medium for the messages I am employed to convey?
- Does its look, tone, feel, graphics, and written content reflect the true image, character, and values of my company?
- Does the publication achieve the organizational objectives set for it?
- Should it be distributed more/less often?
- Does each issue's table of contents reflect those objectives?
- Does the editorial format suit my readers?
- Should I tailor the fit more precisely?
- Is a complete overhaul necessary because the publication is basically incompatible with its targeted audience?
- Does the style suit my particular strengths and skills? If you're an exceptional photographer, for instance, wouldn't it make sense to design your publication to optimally reflect that talent?
- Does my publication attempt the impossible dual task of influencing incompatible audiences?

Getting to Know Them

What enthralls a financial analyst, for instance, isn't likely to turn on a millwright or receptionist, and vice versa. Some editors would make a case for distributing an absorbing employee publication to stockholders rather than providing an externally oriented newsletter or magazine to employees and calling it "their" publication.

Other communicators decry sending internal publications to outside audiences of any kind. Usually it's management that suggests it as a cost-conscious public relations gesture, and the editor who carries out the mistake. Realistically, legislators, opinion leaders, the general public, and executives of related organizations are too busy to wade through even well-written, tightly edited newsletters.

The truth is most external publications have poorly defined goals, the result of little or no editorial planning. Outside audiences must be carefully targeted, and then bagged with the precise communications weapon. Doing that takes a high-powered rifle with a sniper scope, not a scattergun filled with buckshot.

So begin by identifying the primary audience of your newsletter. Make it clear to yourself and to management exactly for whom the publication is intended. Then get to *know* these people, your precious readers, the way you'd thoroughly acquaint yourself with the characters in a novel you were writing.

Find their motivational buttons and when to push them. Learn what makes them tick, what moves, interests, excites, and inspires them. What gets their attention, what loses it quickly, what emotionally turns them on — and off.

Write for readers as the real people they are. Here, too, do journalism's five "W's" and an "H" come into play as you ask yourself:

- *Who* are my readers?
- *Why* is it important for me to know and understand them?
- *What* am I trying to tell them?
- *When* are my best times to communicate on specific subjects?
- *Where* are the best places in my publication to achieve my objectives?
- *How* do I achieve these critical ends?

It will be important, too, to systematically measure your publication's progress in achieving its communications goals — its successes, deficiencies, and failures, using these periodic measurements to improve what you do and how you're doing it. The sooner you learn what you or a previous editor has been getting right, the quicker you can make it better. And fix whatever you're doing wrong.

Vital Measurements

Like their financial counterparts, communications audits gather data about performance to assess its significance. Sound judgments grow from evidence, not hunches. A regular audit measures what your publication achieves, reveals how well it performs, rates your own efforts, and encourages two-way communications.

Audits take such forms as focus groups and selective interviews, but the simplest, most popular organizational tool is the readership survey. It asks the reader questions that elicit easily interpreted answers relative to your communications goals.

Audits cost time, money, and careful planning, but you ought to consider doing one soon if you (1) just took over as editor; (2) recently altered the publication's goals, audiences, or design; (3) have experienced major organizational changes such as rapid growth, geographic relocation, a takeover, or merger; (4) must justify your existence to management; or (5) have not had an audit for more than a year.

The least costly, most efficient way to distribute a readership survey is in the publication to be audited so the two documents can work together. Make the questionnaire easy to fill out and to return, so it ought to be a postcard or a separate form not bound into the publication, with a stamped, addressed envelope.

What You Need to Know

Essentially, what readership surveys try to determine is:

- *Receptivity.* Do your readers like your publication? Do they read it? On the average, how much of each issue do they read?
- *Credibility.* For the most part, do your readers believe what you tell them?
- *Attitude/Behavior Changes.* Does the newsletter affect your readers' attitudes and behavior? The best way to find out is to ask them point-blank. A sample question: What I read in *XYZ News* ( ) often, ( ) sometimes, ( ) never changes my attitude or behavior on specific issues.
- *Recall.* How much of what they read do they remember? Ask them to name past articles and issues they liked or disliked. Avoiding questions with answers that rely on memory is generally good advice because such questions test recall rather than results. But while hard data is important, facts and figures alone rarely tell the whole story. Subjective information can lead to insights that numbers won't suggest, so ask for a few feelings and impressions. People tend to tell you how they really feel when they get a bit emotional.
- *Comprehension.* Is what they read easy to understand? Ask them (gulp!) to evaluate your writing. You might even list the current issue's table of contents and encourage readers to grade each article from "A" to "F" for clarity, credibility, readability, and so on.

Finally, leave your ego out of communication audits. Granted, this is advice easier given than taken. How can it *not* hurt when a publication you've poured your heart and talent into receives a slew of "C" and "D" grades? But remind yourself your efforts reflect not just your skills but those of a team of people. And you're asking your readers for their evaluation and input so you can improve on your collective efforts, not merely to pump up your ego. Still, criticism smarts, no matter how thick the skin it slaps.

Hey, it's OK to get stung occasionally. Learn to take it the right away. You and your publication will benefit from it. Learning from criticism is something you're going to have to accept as a professional writer because there will always be people who don't like what you write. So get over it.

Make It Easy

A few more tips on preparing readership surveys:

Make your questions simple and precise. Leave no room for misunderstanding. After drafting the questionnaire, pretest it on an editorial committee and/or random readers. Evaluate their reactions and edit your questions accordingly.

Don't be greedy. The easier your audit is to complete, the greater will be your readers' response to it, even though a longer questionnaire that garners more information, with less of a return, might be more valuable to you. It's your call. Just don't make replying so tedious that you get a minimal response.

Questions such as these, requiring a simple check-mark should do nicely:

- I usually read ( ) all, ( ) most, ( ) some, ( ) none of *XYZ News.*
- I ( ) usually, ( ) occasionally, ( ) never take the publication home for the family to read.
- I usually believe ( ) everything, ( ) most, ( ) some, ( ) none of what I read in *XYZ News.*
- I think the writing in *XYZ News* is ( ) excellent, ( ) good, ( ) adequate, ( ) bad.
- I think the writing tends to be ( ) too complicated, ( ) about right, ( ) too simple.
- I think the articles are usually ( ) too long, ( ) about right, ( ) too short.
- (Check as many boxes as you consider applicable) I'd like to see more ( ) company news, ( ) industry news, ( ) personality profiles, ( ) department profiles, ( ) safety stories, ( ) retirement benefits information, ( ) other.
- *Solicit opinions.* Even though qualitative evidence is less precise than statistical data, it is not less valid-and may even more useful. So throw in an open-ended question or two asking readers exactly how they feel about the publication. And try not to take the responses personally. Just remind yourself everyone's a critic at heart.

- *Assure anonymity. Don't* ask your respondents to identify themselves. Doing so will only cut your returns. Assure readers only they will know they participated in the audit. However, if it would be helpful (and worth the effort) to determine how many readers respond from each organizational location, you might color-code the forms.

- *Report the results.* Promise a full report on the communications survey in the publication's next issue. This knowledge should impart a proprietary feeling on the part of your readers and, hopefully, elevate the response. Employees will appreciate sharing your findings. And do thank them ahead of time for participating.

- *Don't expect too much.* Few of your readers will feel as strongly about your publication as you do, so don't set yourself up for a major let-down. You'll probably overestimate both the quantity and quality of responses. Again, don't take it personally.

Friends in High Places

Recruit an editorial committee of three to five members of top management or individuals designated by them to help you structure, evaluate, and upgrade each issue of your periodical.

Plan to meet with this group regularly, at least once a quarter, and stay in touch with all the members constantly. Involve them in plotting the course of your publication. Consider them necessary allies, not meddlesome adversaries. Aside from providing you with valuable editorial direction, they just may prove to be the best friends you have in the organization — influential advocates of your cause. And you'll need as many of them as you can get. Beware, however, you don't install road-blocks that impede the efficient, timely issuance of your publication.

Editorial committees have formal functions such as these:

- *They represent management's views and concerns.* Their role is to ensure that the mission statement (a precise definition of the collective purpose of everyone working for the organization) is correctly interpreted and implemented in all internal and external communications endeavors.

• *They help determine reader needs,* assisting you in finding out exactly what your readers want and require in the way of editorial content.

• *They help evaluate input from readership surveys* and other forms of communication audits-aiding you in pinpointing deficiencies in filling reader needs.

• *They help develop editorial plans,* helping you draft long-range goals and the publication's tables of contents to achieve them.

• *They help secure copy approvals,* aiding you in minimizing bottlenecks and meeting publication deadlines.

INTERNAL PUBLICATION OBJECTIVES

A typical employee magazine's communication objectives:

• Foster and promote an understanding of organizational objectives, operations, procedures, services, benefits, programs, and mission.

• Facilitate an exchange of ideas and information between employees.

• Acknowledge and publicize the exceptional service and achievements of employees within the company and local community.

• Provide information on pensioners' activities and achievements.

• Promote health and safety practices.

• Foster a positive employee and organizational attitude and spirit.

• Inform and entertain.

EXTERNAL PUBLICATION OBJECTIVES

A typical external publication's communications objectives:

• Support company goal of remaining the preferred supplier of our services and products.

• Provide customers with information on company programs and services that will enable them to use our products wisely and efficiently.

• Increase public understanding of the price and value of our company services.

• Stress quality of service.

• Explain rate changes.

• Show how company is working to maintain a large customer base to help spread fixed costs.

• Explain basis of prices/fees/rates.

• Increase public awareness of the company's concern for customers. -Write about company efforts to help the disadvantaged.

• Show customers how we optimize the benefits of our products.

• Increase public awareness of the company as innovative and well-run.

• Demonstrate how cost-savings measures are implemented and optimized.

• Show how company uses new technologies to provide more efficient, cost-effective services.

• Show how company is committed to advancing minorities in its work force.

• Show how development programs benefit all customers.

• Increase public awareness of company and its employees as responsible members of the community.

• Show human side of company by writing about employees' civic contributions and volunteer activities.

• Publicize commitment to improving educational opportunities for students in organization's communities and service territories.

• Evidence company's concern for preserving the environment.

• Increase public awareness of the company's commitment to providing the highest quality products and services.

• Define corporate training programs.

• Reveal new technologies designed to improve safety, improved quality-control programs, and research and development efforts.

CHAPTER 10

SETTING YOUR PUBLICATION'S STYLE

Most of this book deals with literary style: The personality, charisma, and visceral appeal of your writing. But this chapter focuses on another aspect of style, spelled with a lowercase "s" as in stylebook: The rules, standards, and guidelines governing consistent usage, proper grammar, punctuation, spelling, and capitalization of the language in your publication.

Here, consistency is paramount.

Here, style relates not so much to your choice of words as the manner in which you use them consistently.

"There is little difference between a Martini and a martini," notes *The New York Times* news editor Lewis Jordan in his newspaper's *Manual of Style and Usage,* "but unless there is a style rule, the word may be capitalized in one instance and lowercased in another."

Such untidiness must be avoided in matters small and large, chides Jordan, because it detracts from even the best of writing. "Rules are especially needed when many very different people write and edit a publication that has an identity of its own."

Rather than draft a style guide of their own, most communicators purchase guiding texts as their editorial bibles. *The New York Times Manual of Style and Usage, The Associated Press Stylebook and Libel Manual, The Modern Language Association Style Book*, the *Government Printing Office Style Book*, and *Chicago Manual of Style* are a few respected primers on the market.

Roll Your Own

Borrowing from these and other manuals, some organizational editors create their own communication canons, which, come to think of it, isn't a bad way to impress the boss.

Do-it-yourself stylebooks run the gamut from acceptable to impressive. Aside from the usual directives on proper usage and related topics, some homegrown manuals include tips on taking pictures, conducting interviews, writing captions, and editing copy.

Others contain bibliographies, publication objectives, pep talks for corporate correspondents, guidelines to avoid ethnic and sexual stereotyping, instructions on securing approvals before forwarding copy, even "readability formulas" and "fog indexes" to encourage organizational writers to rate and improve their copy's "user-friendliness," in the words of one Midwestern newsletter editor.

By all means, assemble your own style guide as you see fit, but take Nike's ad slogan to heart and just do it. Then implement your handbook with the conviction that the key to grammatical harmony, as in marriage, is devotion to an unimpeachable source.

Let it be your first and final arbiter in all matters within its jurisdiction, for stylistic cohesion is critical to your newsletter's credibility and success.

And not sticking to one set of resource guides will almost assure you a stylistically ragged publication. The only way you will achieve editorial uniformity is to select *one* stylebook, *one* dictionary, even one almanac and encyclopedia. Because not all reference guides are created equal. Far from it. They are as variegated in temperament and opinion as individual writers and editors.

A Guideline for Everything

In the writing, editing, and typesetting of each issue, endless considerations will surface concerning grammar, punctuation, capitalization, and typographic design. These are guidelines which should all be in place. Will you, for instance, abbreviate or spell out all components of addresses, dates, titles, states, and so on? And what is the acceptable format for each?

What about numbers and fractions? Will you omit commas before "Jr." and "Sr." and Roman numerals in names? Are you certain which punctuation marks appear inside quotes and which appear outside? How do you set off a state name in a newspaper title?

What about apostrophes? *The New York Times* mandates their use in forming the plurals of letters and numerals: p's and q's, size 7's, B-52's and the 1980's.

But the *Associated Press Stylebook* prefers the deletion of apostrophes, which works fine in the case of numerals and capital letters but can lead to ambiguity when lowercase letters are involved. For instance: "Mind your p's and q's."

In regard to apostrophes tacked onto singular words ending in *s*, such as James and Charles, the *The New York Times* gets a bit more complicated. "Almost all singular words ending in "s" require another "s" as well as the apostrophe to form the possessive," mandates the paper. Thus it's James's book, Charles's hat.

Additionally, the "*s*" after the apostrophe is dropped "in certain expressions in which the word following the apostrophe begins with *s*," as in for conscience' sake, for appearance' sake, for goodness' sake.

The New York Times Manual of Style and Usage also decrees that when two or more sibilant sounds precede the apostrophe, the *s* after the apostrophe is dropped, hence: Kansas' Governor, Moses' behalf.

But what about Bill Parcells? The "c" in his name is as sibilant as the "s" in Moses and Kansas; yet, following the 1991

Super Bowl, a *New York Times* reporter wrote, "He thinks he understands Parcells's message..."

It would be simpler to form the possessive of all words ending in "s" — be they singular or plural, sibilant or not — by placing an apostrophe at the end of *every* word and not dropping the "s" whenever the following word begins with an "s".

Do it for consistency's sake, appearances' sake, for goodness' sake, for Moses' sake, for Bill Parcells' sake, even for *The New York Times'* sake.

As for periods, *The Times* instructs their insertion into abbreviations of company and organizational names (A.T.&T., A.F.L.-C.I.O., C.P.A.) while the *Associated Press* does not: AT&T, AFL-CIO and CPA. Yet, interestingly, the *Times* also drops its periods when abbreviating the names of the network stations: ABC, CBS, NBC.

To the *The New York Times'* sportswriters, "ballcarrier" is one word. But it's "ball carrier" to Associated Press reporters. *The Times* hyphenates 'ball-point" while AP editors don't. And *The Times* advises spelling "brazil nut" all lowercase, while *Webster's Ninth New Collegiate Dictionary* lowercases the nut but capitalizes its country of origin. And we're not even out of the B's (or is it the Bs?) yet.

Go figure for yourself. Then draw up your own rules. Just be consistent applying them. You'll be OK.

Know Before You Need To

E. B. White along with the *Chicago Style Manual* espouses the use of serial commas in sentences that list three or more elements: "Red, white, and blue." "Gold, silver, or copper." "He opened the letter, read it, and made a note of its contents."

The Associated Press Stylebook and Libel Manual, on the other hand, advises omitting the comma before the conjunction in a simple series: "He saw Foote, Cone and Belding on Madison Avenue." "Give me wine, women and song."

One exception is when an integral segment of the series begs a conjunction for clarity: "I had orange juice, toast, and ham and eggs for breakfast."

Another is when a series of complex phrases or independent clauses are strung together: "The main points to consider are whether the athletes are skillful enough to compete, whether they have the stamina to endure the training, and whether they have the proper mental attitude."

You'll note, for instance, that the text of this book follows the *Chicago Style Manual* recommended method of inserting serial commas, unlike many of the examples lifted from newspapers and magazines. The serial comma is considered old-fashioned these days and has fallen into disuse except in publishing circles, in line with the current thinking that the fewer punctuation marks tacked onto a sentence, the less wind-resistant, the more aerodynamic the sentence becomes.

But that's not a good-enough reason for you to abandon the serial comma if you're comfortable using it. That's strictly your call. Just be consistent about it, for the small, nagging inconsistencies in style will erode your credibility and professionalism.

Hence, the need for specific guidelines to assure uniformity, especially when a number of writers contribute to the publication. There's usually no problem when the copy channels through a capable editor, who shapes each issue's editorial melange into a cohesive form. It's the rudderless publication that drifts perilously out to sea.

Caps or Lowercase?

What's your policy on capitalizing titles: business, professional, academic, legislative, military, royal, religious, or whatever? What's your preference on their abbreviation? *(The Associated Press Stylebook* takes almost two whole pages to list the proper ways to capitalize and to abbreviate the military ranks in the U.S. branches of service.)

What about the use of courtesy titles after introducing names? What's your policy on honorifics such as Dr., Mr., Mrs., Miss, and Ms.?

If you choose to emulate *The New York Times,* and few newspapers and magazines do these days in this regard, you'll want to study the newspaper's style manual, which devotes nearly three pages to detailing the acceptable usage of salutatory references. (Ms., by the way, is relegated by *The Times* strictly to quoted matter, letters to the editor, and passages discussing the term itself.)

On the subject of business and occupational titles, virtually all newsstand magazines and newspapers choose *not* to capitalize them, regardless of the context in which they appear. *The New York Times* rules curtly on the matter: "Do not capitalize (company) titles."

The rationale, perhaps, is that such capitalization would smack of homage, a consideration not applied to military, religious, legislative, or other VIP's. The concern may be that business people pay the newspaper's vital advertising revenues and deference to them might appear unseemly.

Conversely, organizational editors flaunt their respect for all executives and employees by capitalizing every title in the publication. The policy is perfectly understandable — and acceptable — as long as strict adherence to one style is maintained. Consistency is critical.

Standardize, Standardize

The *Associated Press Stylebook* offers these guidelines on capitalizing and lowercasing titles:

Capitalize formal titles used directly before one or more names: Pope Paul, President George Washington, Vice Presidents John Jones and William Smith.

Lowercase and spell out titles set off from a name by commas, whether or not the title precedes or follows the name: "The controller, Fred Flackman, was last seen in La Paz,

Bolivia." "Lem Fleeger, the company's sales manager, does not plan to retire."

Lowercase and spell out titles not used with an individual's name: "The public relations manager finally issued a statement." "The quality control manager will not comment."

Lowercase titles that serve primarily as occupational descriptions: astronaut John Glenn, movie star John Wayne, golf course designer Pete Dye.

The various stylebooks provide esoteric variations to these four rules, and you should establish your own basic policy on capitalizing titles. To assure yourself of all-important consistency, I'd suggest simplifying matters even more by routinely capitalizing (or lowercasing) *all* business titles, whether or not they precede the accompanying names.

By indiscriminately capitalizing all titles, you accord all titles due and equal respect. And the policy will avert the danger of one day lowercasing the president/chief executive officer's title because it happens to follow her name while capitalizing the assistant office manager's title because it happens to precede his name.

Speaking of goodwill, *Webster's Ninth New Collegiate Dictionary* — the official dictionary of the Associated Press and most American newspapers — spells it as one word. But good will becomes two words when used as a noun, instructs *The New York Times* style manual, while hyphenated when used as an adjective. The *Associated Press* stylebook concurs on making it two words when used as a noun but rules it an unhyphenated word when used as an adjective.

Who's right? Don't worry about it. As Herman Melville points out, "Who's to doom when the judge himself is dragged to the bar?" Choose for yourself, as long as your usage is consistent.

Consistency Is Critical

Go with the resource guide of your choice. But be loyal to it.
And when you disagree with the dictionary or style guide you
choose — if "goodwill," for example, doesn't look correct to you
as one word, no problem: Make it an exception to the rule. And
be as consistent with your exceptions as you are with your
rules.

On to hyphens. About the size of aphids in a rose garden,
they can be an effective device in revitalizing clichés ("She gave
him one of those
if-looks-could-kill-you'd-be-as-stiff-as-yesterday's-pizza
glares."). Their misuse, however, usually through an obvious
absence, can be as distracting as a handful of chiggers, even to
hardened editors.

Use a hyphen, counsel the experts:

When its omission would cause ambiguity: "The seminar was for
small-business managers." (Without the hyphen in this case the
meaning of the sentence would be unclear.) Other examples:
"He recovered the ball in the outfield." "He recovered his bare
head in the hot sun."

Never force your reader to backtrack, however briefly, to
ascertain your meaning. Someone recovering his head in the
sun would merit a double take — not on the beach but certainly
in the middle of your copy.

When a compound modifier precedes a noun: first-half scores,
gray-green eyes, a hands-full situation, know-it-all man,
better-qualified woman. Exceptions to this rule, advises the
Associated Press, are "very" and other adverbs ending in "ly"
because they naturally lead readers to the modified noun: very
filling food, carefully laid plans.

On another page of the AP style guide, without explanation,
appears a hyphenated "hurly-burly," but a check of *Webster's
New Collegiate* shows the word to be a noun, meaning uproar or
tumult. Hurdy-gurdy is also hyphenated and is likewise a noun,

identifying one of various mechanical musical instruments such as the barrel organ.

The *New York Times* concurs on "ly" endings, but only in regard to adverbs, advising that adjectives ending in "ly" take a hyphen when modifying a noun: gravelly-voiced, grizzly-maned, fuzzily-depicted.

Again, why not simplify matters and assume that an "ly" ending on both adjectives and adverbs sufficiently propels readers to the following word?

But in every case in which the descriptive phrase comes *after* the noun, omit the hyphen: centers for retarded children, not retarded-children centers; cars capable of high speed, not high-speed cars; balloons lighter than air instead of lighter-than-air balloons.

Linking Information

When a "suspensive" device is needed to link units of information. Examples: "The judge gave him a 20- to 30-year sentence." "Minnesotans are used to three-, five-, and nine-inch snowfalls." "Oregonians are both sun- and rain-worshippers." Because a space follows the initial hyphenations, however, suspensive hyphens should be checked thoroughly in type proofs.

When the absence of a hyphen would form a word that appears confusing at first glance, such as anti-intellectual, shell-like (instead of antiintellectual, shelllike).

To designate dual heritage as in the case of Italian-American, Mexican-American and Anglo-American. But *not,* says the AP stylebook, when Latin Americans and French Canadians are involved. *Webster's New International Dictionary* reminds us, though, that "Latin American" is not hyphenated as a noun but is hyphenated as a compound adjective.

Webster's Ninth New Collegiate Dictionary ducks the issue by omitting reference to Latin Americans entirely despite listing "Anglo-American," "Anglo-Catholic," "Anglo-French," "Anglo-Norman" and "Anglo-Saxon," making it clear in every instance that the dual-designations are hyphenated as both nouns and adjectives. Inexplicably, the same volume lists "French Canadian" as a noun but not as an adjective.

To form two-thought compounds such as "serio-comic" and "socio-economic," says the Associated Press. Yet, *Webster's New Collegiate* carries both these listings as one word. So, once again, take your pick.

These inconsistencies in resource guides have been ferreted out to make a point about fallibility. Again, therefore, evaluate the available texts, and then make your own choice based on your writing temperament and philosophy.

Who Knows?

And don't worry about being judged wrong (by whose standards?) as much as being consistent. With our language in constant flux and its learned custodians in perennial disagreement, the limits of correct English usage have become elastic to the point of flaccidity.

The rules of grammar and punctuation change so much and so quickly that, aside from a few inviolate precepts, what is right is simply what works best for each of us in our respective endeavors as organizational writers, novelists, reporters, academicians, politicians, adcrafters, flacksters, or whomever.

When you get right down to it, isn't that the essence of expository writing — employing whatever style is necessary to communicate with our audiences? If no one can say anymore with any amount of legitimacy what is stylistically right or wrong, does it matter whether you shift style from publication to publication, or even from issue to issue, as long as you cleave to one set of rules at a time? Not really, as long as your readers come first and above all other considerations.

To your myriad rules and guidelines, therefore, add one overriding commandment: THOU SHALT NOT IMPEDE THY READERS' PROGRESS. If they must pause, or halt, or back up to catch the drift of your meaning, then you have failed.

Whatever causes readers to lose track of what you're saying — be it stylistic inconsistencies, grammatical flaws, too little punctuation or too much, oversimplication, extreme stylization, dogged adherence to archaic correctness — for whatever reason your words call attention to themselves and away from the message, however briefly — well, then, change them.

Again, good writing is writing that is read — effortlessly, willingly, gratefully, or even grudgingly, but *read*.

CHAPTER 11

SOUP TO NUTS:
SERVING ALL PALATES

Comparing your organizational publication to a dining emporium is appropriate to a discussion on how to cook up appetizing, easily digested magazines and newsletters. Whether your publication equals a five-star restaurant presenting gourmet cuisine, or an all-night beanery with a traditional blue-plate special, or a mom-and-pop café dispensing a sensible selection of wholesome fare at reasonable prices, the analogy fits.

All restaurants have a menu, as does your magazine or newsletter in the form of a table of contents. Restaurants have one or more chefs or cooks and helpers as does your magazine in the form of writers, editors, and correspondents. And most literary fare, like food, can be made more appetizing, easier to swallow.

Food for Thought

Most newsletter copy, like restaurant food, assumes a number of guises, some more tasty than others. Call it food for thought: main courses consisting of news stories and features complemented by a buffet of appetizers, soups, salads, pastas, vegetables, rice or potatoes, breads, desserts, and assorted flavorings such as hot and cold sauces, garnishes, jellies, jams, condiments, and spices.

Not all of these editorial staples need be on your menu, however. Some of the ingredients may be too rich, too varied, too bland, or spicy, or otherwise unsuited to the tastes of your particular clientèle. Then again, a few more dishes, tidbits, and garnishes might serve to perfect your presentation.

Ask yourself:

Is my selection varied enough?

Is it fast-food or gourmet?

Empty caloried or nutritious?

Filling as well as tasty?

All fluff and no substance?

Would my readers welcome more choices?

A few more main courses?

More editorial starch and protein?

Some lighter fare?

More side dishes?

Some hors d'oeuvres?

Desserts?

Fruit to cleanse the palate?

As the checklist indicates, let the form fit the content. A newsletter can be simple or sophisticated, plain or fancy, a balsa glider or a Boeing 747. There are many editorial ways to fly. It all depends on what the editor builds into the superstructure. Let's look at some possible elements.

News Stories

"News" in the form of several paragraphs to a few pages is anything of immediate importance to members of an organization. Content-wise these items run the gamut from reports on corporate, manufacturing, and industry breakthroughs and key events; to sales earnings, business milestones, and marketing trends; to announcements of new products, programs, and policies; to legislative and social developments that exert impact on the newsletter's constituency. And just about everything in-between.

Usually interesting only to members, organizational news stories in organizational publications are written primarily to inform, with little attempt to imbue them with any style or spirit. Don't follow suit.

News Flashes

Some editors introduce late-breaking and less-important news in capsule form — one- and two-sentence bursts that can be graphically highlighted or strung together or scattered throughout the publication as fillers.

Feature Articles

When important enough, features can be lead stories, offering an in-depth look at the inside workings of organizations, key players, and their influence on the outside world. With their dual purpose of entertaining while informing, feature pieces are usually planned and prepared well-ahead of their publication dates in support of long-term objectives.

Sidebars

Providing visual diversity and textual relief, sidebars are usually shorter, self-contained entities complete with headlines, leads, and developed texts that explore subjects relevant to the news or feature articles they support. Typically set off by a box-rule or other graphic device, sidebars also comprise pertinent names and addresses or other secondary information in the form of bibliographies, quotes, events, quotations, or anecdotes that serve to expand and illuminate the central piece.

Pull Quotes

The term "pull quote" identifies quoted material lifted in whole or in part from the text of an article and set off on the page, usually in larger display type. Also known as blurbs, consisting of a handful of words to several sentences, pull quotes fill space, add visual interest, intrigue readers, and give star billing to your story's best quotes. Since these prominently displayed words are accorded proper attribution in the body of the copy, editorial license condones the omission of surrounding quotation marks.

Headlines and Kickers

Not merely arrangements of display type from which to dangle text, headlines are what lure readers into a piece, into the lead paragraph at least. Heads, therefore, are every bit as important as leads, warranting as much creative expression as the body of text that follows. Also, readers who aren't interested in perusing the entire article rely on heads and subheads (kickers) to convey the gist of the story that follows. Additionally, these components serve as graphic elements that can visually dress up a page.

The definition "headline" or "head" is self-explanatory, but you may not be familiar with "kicker" as used in this context. The word refers to the copy positioned just above or immediately below the headline. Varying from a few words to a few sentences, kickers amplify the information provided by the head. Strong kickers should meet the same criteria as powerful headlines, and the best can stand on their own even though their role is to support the head.

Some guidelines on sharpening these key elements of your publication:

Pair strong nouns with active verbs.

Write short, punchy phrases containing no unnecessary words.

Keep verbs in the present tense.

As a rule, omit the articles "a," "an," and "the."

Avoid abbreviations, acronyms, hyphenated words, and awkward splits in phrases and verb constructions.

Be original.

Remember that the dual function of heads and kickers is to inform as they snag attention. They should work together seamlessly to propel readers headlong into the story. Some examples:

Sex and the Single Investor

Your heart is pounding. Your pulse is racing. You're not making love, you're buying stocks.

o

Take a Hike

Sometimes the best thing you can do on the job is to leave it — temporarily.

o

Fresh Start: No Ifs, Ands or Butts

Several Best Western employees have accepted the Challenge of improving their health by joining "Fresh Start," a stop-smoking program.

o

Headquarters Is Spaced Out

Space at headquarters is at a premium, says Dan Silashki, manager of Administrative Services.

o

It's Jim — not Norman...

Mother Didn't Own a Motel.

Here's a gem from *The New York Times Magazine:*

Heck's Angels

They're the mild ones, kickin' tires and quotin' Scripture. Christian biker gangs eat a lot of Big Macs and dust as they ride their Harleys and Hondas for Jesus.

And one from Fortune:

Read This or We'll Cut Off Your Ears

U.S. companies are spending $1 billion a year to protect top executives and their families from terrorists and other attackers. Many don't see the threat realistically.

Note how each kicker immediately amplifies its headline. But kickers aren't always necessary, only when headlines need help. Many succeed quite well on their own, as did this one in a feature piece on a company electrician who excels in barefoot skiing:

Man Puts Body, Sole Into Water

Eye-catching and filling, this newsletter article headline on nutritional eating:

Bacon. Hot Dogs. Pizza. Popcorn. Sausage. Buttered Rolls. Ice Cream. Spare Ribs Peanut Butter. Doughnuts.

Subheads

Placed strategically within the body of an article, subheads signal demarcations in thought while providing visual relief to solid blocks of text. Like other copy, subheads can be imaginative or mundane, but are usually the latter, since most organizational writers simply lift key words from the text to communicate the scope of the succeeding copy. And that's OK. Readers don't expect subheads to be deathless prose. Still, sprightly subheads can lift your publication above the ordinary if you're inclined to make the extra effort.

Captions

Like subheads, captions tend to be prosaic, taken-for-granted appendages to newsletter photos and illustrations. Their main purpose is to identify individuals and the action frozen in time by the photographer or artist. Nonetheless, they can be made to work much harder than they usually do.

At their worst, captions are laughable, the words mimicking the image, yet inane, redundant captions are predictable staples of most organizational publications. Typical examples:

Under the photo of a woman presenting a manual of sorts to a man, both of them grinning as if the object were an academy award, appears the classic caption: "Patricia Plenge presents operating manual to Ken Palumbo."

Under a photo showing two corporate librarians who appear to be checking in books, the caption informs: "Sandi Hopkins checks in books with Georgia Rodeffer."

Alongside the shot of a woman holding a telephone at a desk, a caption reveals: "Carla Sykes speaks on the phone at her desk."

How much less superfluous this *New York Times* caption, appearing under the photo of a huge bear: "A grizzly bear. If attacked by one, don't run; climb a tree or play dead."

An effective way to enliven such captions, particularly when they appear under individuals in common poses, is to append a quote to the name. Forget about a caption under a photo of an employee holding a phone that informs readers it is "Carla Sykes on the phone at her desk." This would be better:

> Carla Sykes: "I'm here to satisfy the customer, whatever his complaint. That's my number one job."

Or follow the lead on this caption, which complemented a typical "mug shot" in a consumer newsletter:

> According to CDFA's Wells, "There is absolutely no evidence that independent testing increases safety. It doesn't turn up anything different from what we find."

Avoid redundancy in your captions by focusing on the "why" of the photo instead of its "what." The *what* is usually obvious. The *why* can be informative and interesting.

Whether or not captions accompany photos and visuals that are integral to an article or which stand alone, make them do some real work by providing lively supplemental information.

This caption from an employee newspaper really earns its keep:

> Baby Boom. New babies have been a constant topic of conversation in the Valve Department at Golden Valley. Since last September, eight new children and grandchildren have been born to employees in that department. The proud folks pictured here, in the front row, left to right, are: Gladys Rettman who has a new grandson and new dads, David Walton who has a new daughter and Gil Rodriguez who added a son to his family. The grandparents in the back row, all with new

granddaughters, arc Marie Hayek, Judy Cokley and Dane) I Spohn. Two grandmothers not pictured, Janis Frank and Phillis Willis, also have new granddaughters.

There's no rule that says photo captions have to be as terse and literal as possible. They can tell a story and have a personality all their own.

Also, write them in the present tense, as if the action is unfolding in front of the reader. Most editors prefer their captions that way.

Take this example from *Time:* "The van from which the mortars were launched bursts into flames."

At *The New York Times*, however, it's the time of the action depicted that matters so past tense is almost always employed:

Pentagon employees lined up to buy Valentine's Day gifts yesterday at a candy shop at the military complex.

But it's your publication so it's strictly your call. Again, though, always be consistent.

Columns

Columns are a great way to involve readers while providing variety to your table of contents: regular, sporadic, or one-time "guest" appearances in the form of first-person editorial contributions from particularly erudite, humorous, or knowledgeable members of the organization.

Recruit regular columnists at various company locations to develop a following with readers through, say, an employee benefits or health-fitness column. Decide which columns will best help you achieve your organizational objectives.

Q&A's

A popular feature, Q&A's not only provide more variety to your editorial mix, they encourage involvement by members of management. And because creative writing isn't really a consideration with this straightforward format, Q&A's can fill a ready niche in your publication. They're also a comfortable format for readers, who can glean factual information from them by skipping to questions and answers that interest them.

And Q&A's can feature one interviewee at a time or several.

Classified Ads

Don't laugh. Want ads are extremely popular with readers, and quite a few organizational publications are devoting more and more pages to them. *Case Line,* a Steelcase employee newsletter, is one. Typically, a quarter to as much as half the publication consists of want ad listings, entitled "Good Deals."

A recent 24-page issue, for instance, devoted 11 entire pages to listings by employees peddling real estate, automobiles, recreational vehicles, equipment of all sorts capped by four more bulging pages of miscellaneous goods and a final page of "wanted" items. All that seemed to be lacking was a "personals" column, but maybe that's next.

Letters to the Editor

You'll want to encourage your readers to express their opinions in print. Run the constructive letters you receive — not all of them will be publishable. This department could become one of the most compelling sections of your publication.

Fillers

Build an endless supply of fillers (known as "sound bites" in the electronic media) ranging from a few lines to several paragraphs, capable of instantly filling any size hole in your publication. Your graphic designer will love you for it — and reward you with light layouts.

CHAPTER 12

INVOLVING YOUR READERS, WORKING WITH OTHERS

Telling your readers what's happening, what's coming up, what's going down. *Information* is the organizational editor's primary objective, achieved largely with news articles and feature stories. But how well editors succeed in fulfilling three other communications objectives determines their publications' popular and enduring appeal.

Along with informing, organizational editors should also *involve, motivate,* and *entertain* readers. These four goals, particularly the last three, are intimately joined. And as frivolous as the fourth objective may seem, it is actually vital, for when editors fail to entertain their readers, they probably don't involve, motivate, or inform them either.

"Entertainment has acquired an unwarranted pejorative connotation," notes screenwriting professor Richard Walter. "It has come to signify that which is fleeting, superficial, insubstantial. But truly to comprehend the term, a writer could do a lot worse than to check out a worthy dictionary. Therein, entertainment is revealed to enjoy an honorable, venerable tradition. To entertain is to occupy, to hold, to give over to consideration as in 'to entertain a notion.' "

But Walter also points out that to entertain is not solely to *divert,* stressing: "A film [or magazine or newsletter] most certainly should achieve more than that, but it cannot accomplish anything at all unless first of all it entertains."

Let's look at how some organizational communicators achieve their secondary goals of involving, motivating, and entertaining their readers. And how a few editors enhance their primary aim of informing.

Involve by Including

"A surefire way to nurture avid readers," remarks Department of Defense editor Mary Rothgeb, "is to put them *into* your publication." The best way to do that, she advises, is with personality profiles that introduce employees to other employees, sales-support staffs to customers and clients, management to the rank-and-file, and vice versa, features and articles that enable readers to get to know the co-workers and customers who are an integral part of their business or professional world.

"In large corporations," says Rothgeb, "this approach can serve to reduce the vastness of the organization and to bring people closer together by removing a little of the impersonality of the enterprise."

Rothgeb's advice should extend beyond personality profiles to include every other area of the publication, for not enough organizational writers and editors fully exploit their readers' strong desire to encounter themselves and the people they know in the pages of their newsletter or magazine.

In every readers' survey, invariably a major complaint spouts from every division, department, and regional office in the organization: not enough attention is paid us in the corporate publication. So a barometer for success could simply be a body count of employees and customers included in each issue — in meaningful ways, of course.

The most effective organizational publications tend, among other things, to be genuinely interested in the people they serve, up and down the corporate ladder.

Sharing the Limelight

But the trick is to represent your constituency in sincere, non-demeaning fashion — to bestow on the least of these corporate brethren their allotted time in the limelight, their 15 minutes in the sun, which may never come if it doesn't come from you. Therein lies the organizational editor's greatest, most satisfying challenge.

Certainly, the corporate editor's biggest bane is the obligatory "People in the News" section with its interminable roster of appointments, promotions, anniversaries, retirements, new hires, and transfers. Filling these necessary pages — much less enlivening them, is as unrewarding for editors as it is for the employees whose names make up the tedious roll calls that require only tenure in the company for inclusion. These lists constitute the palest of corporate acknowledgments.

Unwilling to relegate the company's least spectacular employees to anonymity, some editors find creative ways to shine the spotlight on people who otherwise would never bask in its bright glow.

Champion International's internal newspaper, *The Wire*, for instance, displays the photograph of a randomly chosen employee on the cover of each issue. Alongside the photo runs a biographical "snapshot" of this employee "personality" of the month, supplemented by a longer profile inside.

Invariably, the editor selects a worker from the company's lesser ranks for the cover portrait. Succeeding issues have starred an Illinois maintenance worker, a Texas junior accountant, a Washington shipping clerk, an Alabama mechanic, a Florida scheduler, a North Carolina instrumentation supervisor, and a California sales representative. Published monthly for the Champion "community," the twelve-page, full-color newspaper usually presents a solid array of company and industry news balanced with softer features touching on a range of human-interest subjects.

Another distinguishing mark of the distinctive employee newspaper is the company division's "logo" that appears under the headline of each article to flag the attention of specific employees to material of special interest to them.

Worth Passing On

Thumbing through organizational publications with an eye out for entertaining ways to corral large numbers of employees into print, I came across these features worth passing along. Perhaps they'll spark a few ideas of your own.

Two features — "Paper People Talk Funny" and "A Language All Their Own" — from separate employee magazines take cartoon-looks at how mill workers talk to each other, in words and gestures distinctively their own. Most businesses, industries, and professions have their own jargon. Does yours merit a feature piece of your own?

Many organizational publications regularly profile valued customers. Too often smarmy in their overly flattering portrayals, such features nonetheless nurture client goodwill as well as acknowledge the contribution of sales and sales service personnel to corporate success. The profiles also impress on plant workers the vital need for unrelenting quality control and product consistency.

Department profiles are invariably well-received. But along with haphazardly featuring clumps of employees, consider describing the firm's manufacturing process while you're at it, as did the editor of one wood products magazine. In an engrossing eleven-part series entitled "Water, Wood, Machines & People," the Boise Cascade editor focused on a key employee in each segment of the operation. Moving from mill to mill, he led his readers through the entire papermaking process, acknowledging the vital presence and contribution of on-site workers in the text and accompanying photos.

The series was so well received it was reprinted as a handout-brochure for customers. But a tragic aside involved the employee chosen for the final installment of the series. A machine tender at the company's mill in Maine, the employee died of a massive coronary three weeks after being interviewed and photographed. With the widow's permission, the magazine piece ran as scheduled, a month after the funeral, with this foreword:

> On the Tuesday morning of May 4, Bill Thornton obligingly came into the mill on his free time to be interviewed for this *Paper Times* profile. That night, shortly after he began his midnight shift, the accompanying photographs were taken. Busily-checking himself out on No. 12 paper machine, he was hardly aware of the camera. Barely three weeks later, as everyone at Rumford knows, he died, the sudden victim of a massive coronary. Most everyone who knew Bill Thornton probably remembers him as he appears in these pictures. It is fitting, therefore, that we publish the article and photos as if he were still machine tender on No. 12. Those closest to him say he would have liked it that way.

Unusual hobbies and interests, civic contributions, individual exploits, and personal accomplishments are obvious, valid reasons to publicize specific employees, either singly or in groups. Such profiles are usually up-beat and popular with readers.

Any editor who thrashes the corporate bushes for these subjects will find coveys of them to feature.

Here are some organizational "personalities" who were introduced to their co-workers with diverting heads and leads:

Caught in a Jam

> When Charles Ware isn't making newsprint at the Lufkin, Texas, mill, he makes something infinitely sweeter at home: jellies and jams. These fruits of his labor are not the usual peanut butter partners. Ware's special blueberry, blackberry and dewberry preserves have earned ribbons at the Texas State Fair every year since 1980.

o

Portrait of an Actress

Last summer, Joan Edwards was a dead mother. Recently, she turned murderer and buried her victims in the basement.

Edwards, an 11-year Champion employee and a secretary in the Sartell, Minnesota, mill's technical department, is a member of the Inverted Pyramid Theater Troupe at the County Stearns Theatrical Company in St. Clouds.

o

K.C. to Gateway in Doghouse's Double-breasted Yamaha

Translated from CB jargon, that means Kansas City to St. Louis in Gene Kratzberg's White Freightliner. What better way to write about a trucker who's driven a million safe miles than to ride with him? A winter storm had dumped four inches on Kansas City the day before, and Gene Kratzberg shielded his eyes against the morning glare coming off the banked snow as he carefully jockeyed his 18-wheeler out of the Boise Cascade parking lot.

o

It's Not Sold Until It's Paid For

Most of the time Elmo Abernathy talks just the way you'd expect a credit manager, law degree holder and part-time college professor to talk, since he is all of these things. But he is also an avid fisherman, who occasionally sounds like any other angler drowning night crawlers in a trout stream, and it is during these conversational lapses that he makes the most sense. Ask him, for instance, to describe the primary functions of his Paper Group credit department and he throws out such jargon as, "We're not part of the traditional corporate financial hierarchy found most elsewhere. Here the credit function is purely a piece of the marketing action. That's a growing contemporary practice across the nation and one that seems to best suit companies with fixed mill capacity and relatively few customers to whom they are principal suppliers. And the Paper Group fits this profile. In effect, we entrust comparatively few customers with vast amounts of money. Therefore, it makes good sense for the credit department to be involved in the preliminary negotiation stages." Then the fisherman emerges: "When you're putting a lot of eggs in a few baskets, you want to make damn sure from the outset that none of the baskets have any holes."

o

A Bloody Good Day at Salem

Blood. If you or a loved one ever need any, better hope there are enough Lewis McRaes in your community. If not, you could be in trouble. And unfortunately he's somewhat of a rarity. For instance, Friday, March 15th was Louie's day off. Yet he came into the Salem mill that afternoon — to give blood. Again. As he's done 73 times before in his life.

No one will argue that it's not desirable to include as many employees as possible — interestingly and meaningfully — in the pages of an employee publication. Stories of the ubiquitous company picnics, retirement parties, and million-safe-hours celebrations are ubiquitous opportunities to portray happy, motivated workers.

But there are many more ways to shepherd rank-and-file employees into your publication — unheralded, hard-working men and women who would remain anonymous without your imaginative efforts to rope them into the organizational spotlight, if only briefly, if only in the pages of your publication.

The following grab-bag of ideas, culled from peer publications, may help you randomly involve employees from the broad base of your organizational pyramid, deserving men and women who would otherwise remain nameless and unrecognized

Contests

The possibilities for contests are endless. Publish stock photos from old movies, as did one editor, who titled his contest "Captions Courageous." In each issue, he ran a stock photo from a vintage movie with a sample caption tailored to his publication's industry and offered a few prizes, inviting readers to submit their own entries.

Stage a "hat" contest, as did another employee-magazine editor, who solicited snapshots of employees sporting their favorite headgear. The resulting feature, titled "The Good, the Bad and the Ugly," showed eleven employees from company installations in Iowa, Maine, Utah, Maryland, Minnesota, Washington, North Carolina, and Texas strutting their winning entries in eleven "hat" categories: Oldest, Most Honest, Most Useful, Dirtiest (this one emblazoned with the epithet "Damn Seagulls"), Most Popular, Biggest, Best Collection, Best Retiree, Best Male Chauvinist Pig (adorned with the snout of — what else?), Friendliest, and Strangest.

Involve Many Readers

The beauty of such contests, especially a series of them, is their ripple effect. They can ensnare any number of readers and their families. Spread the ripples by recruiting five or six employees to judge the entries in each contest, and identify those judges when you announce their choices. Do capsule profiles of the winners, quoting them on how they intend to spend their prize-money.

And since your plan, of course, is to feature as many employees as possible in each issue, well, publish *every* entry you receive, along with the corresponding names and corporate locations, citing all after your winners as "Honorable Mentions."

"Nothing dishonorable in that," remarked the *Paper Times* editor. "I ran the name of every participating employee alongside his or her caption. My first contest brought in seven entries, the second twenty-one, the fourth fifty-seven, and so on. We ran a total of seven contests before switching to something else, and it proved to be one of the magazine's all-time-popular features."

Other editors have found readers responsive to short (fifty* words-or-less) essay contests. You might solicit thoughts on a variety of topics such as "What this country needs is...," "The most unforgettable co-worker I ever met was...," and "If I could run this company for a day, the first thing I would do is..."

Or run a coloring contest for employees' children.

Or put on an Ugly Necktie Competition — a perfect feature for a post-Christmas issue.

Ask readers to send in their most unsightly gift ties. Award first-place, second-place, and third-place prizes for the ugliest ties, then present an ugly tie (someone else's entry) to all runners-up.

Or ask all the kiddies out there to describe what their moms, dads, grandmas, or grandpas do for the company. One editor unveiled such a contest with this catchy headline and kicker:

ANNOUNCING THE "DO YOUR CHILDREN KNOW WHERE YOU ARE TODAY?" CONTEST

What does your son, daughter or grandchild think you do when you go off each day with your lunch bucket or briefcase? Sit the youngster down and have him or her write about it. Earn yourself some prize money through child labor!

Slogans, Photos, Essays

Slogan contests are also effective when they offer an enticing incentive for competing, such as *Sailing Scene* magazine's enticement of "a pair of quality binoculars" for the best original "Let's Go Sailing" slogan. In employee publications, slogan contests effectively heighten awareness of corporate concerns such as job safety, quality control, and plant cleanliness.

Need a new name for your publication? Who better than your readers to come up with one? Run a contest. Reward the winner. And while you're at it, explain what your new publication is all about. The editor of *The Zondervan News* did just that to acknowledge the company's acquisition by a New York publishing house.

One contest and seventy-five submissions later, the publication reached its readers with a new masthead sporting the name suggested by Cheryl Rose of the company's Production Department, who was awarded a $30 meal at her favorite restaurant. The newsletter's new name: *The Zondervan Grapevine.*

The employee photo contest is the granddaddy of them all. Winning entries wind up on cafeteria walls, bedeck virtually entire issues of organizational publications, and even decorate annually-issued full-color company calendars.

A beer company once polled its 20,000 employees on their reaction to receiving an annual photo contest calendar. Of the 1,495 survey cards returned, all but twenty-six (1.7 percent) were positive. "It gives me a sense of corporate pride and feelings of closeness to fellow employees I would otherwise not experience," responded one grateful employee, no doubt delighting the entire communications staff.

That's what it's all about: acknowledging the presence and contributions of employees throughout the organization — not always an easy task when far-flung divisions, branches, plants, sales offices, customers, and constituents are involved.

Self-Expression Always Engaging

A tried-and-true method of involving employees is the reliable worker-on-the-spot feature, in which five or six employees grin at the camera alongside their responses to pithy questions such as "What is your fantasy job?" and "What do you think can be done to improve safety where you work?" It's a pleasant way to systematically represent the organization's scattered locations by highlighting several local workers.

One enterprising editor covers the corporate waterfront by asking on-site communicators to take snapshots — not of interesting faces but of amusing bumper stickers that show up in the company parking lot. The resulting montages of pithy sayings have become a staple of her newsletter.

Another editor asked employees to pass along the messages they encountered on their co-workers' vanity license plates, along with the stories behind these modes of self-expression. The result was an engaging two-page feature that represented employees from a total of fourteen states and eleven company locations.

Others have concocted special recipes to blend disparate individuals with common avocations and interests into editorial pastiches. One editor dug through personnel rosters to whip up an amusing piece on employees with famous names. Another compiled the favorite mottoes of random executives and workers in the company.

Others have done features grouping corporate athletes. *Developments,* Raychem Corporation's employee magazine, ran such a piece, titling it "The Joy of Sweat," in which an ultramarathoner (chemist), a marathoner (engineer), a volleyball player (technical services representative), a softball player (personnel manager), and a competitive swimmer (product marketing director) were profiled together.

A succeeding *Developments* issue told the stories of employees "who are applying their creative talents to unusual hobbies, inventions, and their own small businesses." Aside from recognizing deserving employees, the feature led off with a statement that surely gladdened the CEO's heart:

"Creativity is a highly prized commodity at companies such as Raychem. We hire people who have it; we foster a corporate culture that stimulates and rewards it; and we reap its benefits in the form of new technologies, new manufacturing processes and new markets."

Again, the possibilities are endless, limited only by your fertile imagination. Or someone else's. No need to constantly reinvent the wheel. Get on the mailing list of award-winning publications. Study newsstand magazines. Keep a "swipe" file. Recycle the good ideas you find. Smart editors do, because so little is new these days. But it *can* be to your readers, who are all that matter.

Build a Communications Network

Something else that will matter greatly to you as a communicator is your ability to work well with others in your organization — particularly those in far-away places. They are someplace you aren't and possess something you don't: access to people and events you wouldn't know about without them.

Aside from your writing and editing skills, how effective you are in setting up a network of correspondents — and how persuasively you motivate them — could be paramount to your success. Without enthusiastic support from the field, you may be left with home plate well covered and the other bases wide open.

There's a word critical to all organizational communicators: *Involvement.* You must get other people involved in your communications cause and keep them motivated.

How? Someone once said, "There's no limit to the amount of good you can do if you don't care who gets the credit." That may be well and good for a few shining souls, but the American System is predicated on being rewarded for one's contributions. Apply that principle to managing your communicators. Goodness may be its own reward, but sweeten it with some recognition and a sense of accomplishment. List your regional reporters in the masthead. Even run their pictures alongside their names, as some organizational editors do. Make them "stars" at every opportunity. Most certainly give them a byline whenever it's warranted.

And provide them as many "tools" as possible: an in-house stylebook (a worthwhile document to draft if one doesn't exist); guidelines on the types of news stories and features you're after; "how-to" manuals on improving writing, editing, interviewing, and photography skills. Treat your correspondents as professionals, and they'll reward you in kind.

Remind yourself periodically of one truism of good management: The best way to get others to care is to care yourself. And *show* it.

CHAPTER 13

EVERYTHING I KNOW, WHAT I'LL NEVER UNDERSTAND

Keep one thing in mind as you write, as you edit other people's writing, and whenever you subject your own writing to another's approval: It's not brain surgery. In terms of the cosmos, it isn't even ingrown-toenail repair.

Writing is an inexact, thoroughly subjective, emotional exercise unsuited to precise, scientific evaluation. At its best, it is a magnificent tool to elucidate truth, but it isn't truth itself.

The quality of all writing, therefore, rests strictly in the opinion of the beholder. Whether your writing is good, bad, fair, awful, or magnificent relies, when all is said and done, on one thing: The judgment and approval of the individual with the final say on what gets into print and what doesn't.

Hang onto that thought whenever you're editing or being edited. If you're lucky, it will keep you from taking yourself and you work too seriously. The world and particularly you will benefit immensely from your humility.

Cutting the Cards

In a sand-flea-infested backwater of my youth called Parris Island, South Carolina, I picked up a precept for dealing with others that has held me in good stead throughout my corporate communications career. It's called the 10-percent rule, and I'd like to pass it along to you.

Years ago, at the Marine Corps Recruit Depot where they took my soft, undisciplined body and forged it into a finely tuned fighting machine, a senior drill instructor named Karl Minnick enlightened me on the 10-percenters of the world.

"No matter how often and efficiently you put out the word," he snarled at me one blistering afternoon, eyes livid, breath hot, nostrils flaring centimeters from my quavering features, "10 percent of the troops will never get with the program. Just pray, boy, you're never one of them!"

I've cleaned up his language a bit, but that was the gist of my D.I.'s benign counsel. Many years later, I still carry his words in a velvet pouch suspended in my memory, except that I've made it a 40-percent rule. What Staff Sergeant Minnick meant was that no matter which group of people you ask, beg, bully, or cajole into doing something for you by a certain deadline, you'll average these results:

Three out of ten will deliver promptly, as promised, two of them coming through with flying colors, the third doing a passable job. Two others will get you something barely usable, in the nick of time. Another will FedEx a huge package — eight days too late. And you'll never hear from the other four. Hence the 40-percent rule.

As a writer or editor laboring under a constant deadline, accept as gospel the fact that 40-percenters will always be with us. Factor them into all your endeavors and you'll never work yourself into a frazzle again.

Rule Two of the Communicator's Survival Manual: People who seem too good to be true usually are. Count on them, but not too much. Trust everyone, but cut the cards. Or as an old Slovenian proverb advises, "Pray to God for a good harvest, but keep on hoeing."

Salting Copy with Red Herrings

Many years ago, a highly successful New York advertising copywriter bequeathed me this priceless bit of advice: Never submit perfect copy for approval. Always throw in a few red herrings to be ferreted out, "errors" to be caught, copy to be "improved." Because it takes a saint, he reasoned, not to correct something — anything — when asked to edit copy. Leave in some rough sentences, he counseled, a weak phrase or two, even some typos to divert attention from the good stuff. Call it editorial quality control.

On Giving a Damn for Credibility

You start with a "damn." If no one suggests changing it to "gee," next time try "hell." If that mild expletive slips through the editorial gauntlet, go for a "(bleep)." Not the pungent word usually displaced by a bleep, mind you, just "(bleep)" itself, to acknowledge the fact that there are people in the world, some — mercy! — in your own employ, who occasionally salt their conversations with such piquant expressions.

But why? Not to offend your readers' sensibilities, but for credibility's sake which, like excellence, is often achieved with attention to realistic detail — such as having people converse in print the way they do in real life. Mind you, I'm not advocating crude language for its own sake or as regular fare in organizational publications despite the fact that crudity of expression is common in today's movies, newsstand publications, television programming, and everyday conversations.

When the older President Bush, for instance, informed a Congressional group several days before Christmas of 1990 that Saddam Hussein was "going to get his ass kicked" if war broke out in the Persian Gulf, every news medium in the country carried his words verbatim. *Newsweek* prefaced the quote with one by the late columnist Joseph Alsop about John F. Kennedy: "A Stevenson with balls." In a subsequent issue, the same news weekly included in its report on "G.I. gulf-speak" a term allegedly used by soldiers on the front line to describe those who aren't: "REMFs — Rear Echelon Mother – – – – ers."

I'm not suggesting we're anywhere close to publishing such ribald comments and references in organizational publications, maybe everywhere else in this permissive age. There are times, however, in corporate communications when credibility relies on portraying people as they really are, talking the way they actually speak.

This point was dramatized in a powerful employee magazine feature on recovering alcoholics at a paper mill in Maine. What distinguished the piece were the employees who volunteered to be photographed and tell their stories to their co-workers in their own hard-hitting words.

One of the six courageous mill workers was quoted in this fashion: "'How far is it to Augusta? Two six-packs,' I used to tell people. Your whole life revolves around that (bleeping) bottle!"

Later on in the article, the only member of the group who hasn't been divorced is offered a compliment on his wife: "She must be quite a woman." He replies: "Hell, she's a (bleeping) saint!"

Using the "f" adjective in these instances would have been perfectly natural, but the organizational writer didn't try it, he confesses with a resigned grin, "because that's not going to happen in my corporate communications lifetime. But at least someone didn't change 'Hell, she's a (bleeping) saint!' to 'Oh, yes, she's a positive joy.'

"And only we in corporate communications," the writer adds laughingly, "know what small victories like that really mean."

So the "damns" and "hells" and "(bleeps)" in organizational print aren't ends in themselves but means to a greater goal, which is simply management's concession to its editors that no subject, if it is of sufficient concern to readers and treated intelligently, will be taboo in an organizational publication.

Your newsletter's credibility relies on whether or not you avoid bad news and on how you present matters of contention and delicacy. The manner in which you write — or don't write — about subjects that stir emotion, foster debate, and incur disagreement can make or break your publication.

What happens too often in corporate communications is that employees walk around under a miasma of impending doom and pessimism while the people who can — and should — clear things up pretend nothing out of the ordinary has happened.

Sensitive, controversial topics in print do tend to frighten management. But for the sake of credibility, organizational editors should be allowed to relate disappointing news, soften corporate blows, and explain unpopular management decisions — without whitewash or condescension.

Even if it means an occasional (bleep), for G–d's sake.

On Being Mr. or Ms. Goodboss

There are shelves full of books on how to become a good editor, a better manager, a wonderful human being. And to all this profound advice, let me add my own humble thoughts on the qualities and characteristics that distinguish the exceptional organizational editor and communication manager:

Mr. and Ms. Goodboss allow you to fail. In fact, they regard failure as a prerequisite of accomplishment, part of the overhead of success. Mr. or Ms. Badboss, on the other hand, will not tolerate it, even at the expense of never succeeding. And not allowing you to fail means you won't get the chance to succeed — even though your success would be Badboss's achievement too. But so would your failure, you see, so Badboss prefers to forgo the former rather than risk the latter. The difference between the two bosses is that one attempts to make things happen, to precipitate change, and to effect progress. Goodboss is willing to rock the boat if it means getting somewhere. Badboss gets seasick at the thought.

Goodbosses are secure in their own talents, abilities, and contributions — and not intimidated by yours. As a result, Goodbosses encourage and take pride in your efforts and accomplishments.

Confronted with your ideas and projects, Goodbosses occasionally asks "Why?" but usually "Why not?" And with this consent, they bequeath control to you — ah, the luxury and rarity of it.

Goodboss recognizes, particularly in regard to writers and editors, that the biweekly paycheck, no matter how enriching, is minor compared to the intangible rewards of the job — a sense of achievement, satisfaction, and the personal growth that comes from reaching. So he or she gives people the precious room to stretch their skills and talents.

Goodboss's antitheses — unfortunately, there are many more of them than Goodbosses — are the (Boo!) editors from hell. Like aliens from outer space, usurping human bodies and scrambling their brains into Hamburger Helper, they're out there, turning organizational writers into blithering idiots.

Running Editorial Gauntlets

Beware, as well, these unholy members of organizational copy-approval gauntlets (worse, becoming one of them yourself):

The Multi-headed Decision Maker. Ask any grizzled organizational writer for whom he'd rather work — a tyrannical editor with a clear, if twisted, image of the end-product and the stamina to shepherd that vision into print? Or one who bases all decisions on the collective opinion of a committee of pleasant, conscientious, considerate Alphonses and Gastons, each achingly respectful of the other's editorial tastes and opinions.

It's like asking an NFL kicker if he'd prefer trying to convert from 60 yards out — or from 5 yards away with the uprights in constant motion. No doubt, most kickers would opt for the longer range but unwavering goalposts. For both groups of professionals, the most frustrating thing in the world is a moving target. And approval committees usually provide just that.

A good lesson for organizational editors to learn early is to keep their editorial gauntlets to a minimum. Involve others (such as editorial committees) to secure direction — but early in the process. Editing is *one* person's job — the editor's.

The Dental Yentl. This most cautious of editors methodically extracts every fang, tusk, molar, bicuspid, and incisor from the jaws of every communications project he or she is handed —

ensuring that nothing with teeth will ever bite back. Dental Yentls approve no copy with the slightest potential for offending anyone.

The motto on this editor's desk: "We've always done it that way. And we always will." The status is irrevocably quo. Innovation and creativity are not appreciated, for they bring newness in their wake, thus unpredictability. You say you'd like to redesign the old newsletter that's looked the same for the past twenty years. (*"Why?"* is the predictable reply.) You say it'll only cost a few hundred dollars, a grand max, to hire a professional designer to lay out a bold, dramatic, new format. (*"What?!"*) End of discussion.

And humor is strict verboten to the Dental Yentl: "What's funny to one person can be offensive to another!" Negativism in any form is also a no-no ("Always be positive!"). Even grammatical license is forbidden ("What was good enough for my fourth grade English teacher..."). The only trouble with rendering all your copy toothless is that, while it may never snap back at you, it won't sink its teeth into anyone else's consciousness either.

Challenges don't stir this intrepid editor's blood, they merely upset his stomach.

The Spruce Gooser. This editor tries to build every balsa glider into a Spruce Goose (Howard Hughes' eight-engine wooden flying boat that got airborne just once — for a mile at a maximum height of 70 feet — before its retirement to a Long Beach museum). The Spruce Gooser's proud motto: "I improve everything. Whether it needs it or not."

Endlessly, they fix things that aren't only not broke but work beautifully, tacking, splicing, grafting wings, organs, limbs, and myriad appendages onto everything they're given to inspect. Then they give it back to you to fly. "Simplicity" is not a word in the Spruce Gooser's vocabulary. Working with such an editor is like taking a stroll around the block that winds up a safari with 40-pound packs up and down the slopes of Mt. Kilimanjaro.

The Great Amender. This first cousin of the Spruce Gooser lacks the talent to create anything worthwhile, so he or she does the next best thing: "improve" everyone else's ideas and copy. With a vengeance. Armed with a little knowledge about a great many things — just enough to be dangerous — the Great Amenders wouldn't be destructive if they were only smart enough or trusting enough or secure enough in their own abilities to defer to the talents of the specialists in their employ.

The Mole. "Each of us is the sum total of our experiences," an organizational writer prefaced her views on a particularly unpalatable editor she once worked for. "The greater, more varied those experiences, the broader our outlook on life, and the freer our acceptance of innovative problem-solving. I call him the mole," she explained, "because of this individual's tunnel vision — an extremely narrow perception of the world that he imposes on everyone he employs. And every thing that falls outside the purview of that restricted vision is acutely discomforting, immediately suspect, and ultimately unacceptable."

Pity the moles. But pity the people who report to them even more.

New Buzzwords an Oxymoron

If you must use them, do it while they're fresh. Like bumper stickers, they can be fun when encountered the first one or two times. Then they get old: "Trickle down," "supply side," "magic of the marketplace," "accountability," "empowerment," "segue," "ratchet," "scenario," "schmooze," "paradigm," "tipping point," "whopping" (from the transitive verb "to whop"?).

Use them if you must, but abandon them before they get to be clichés. Nothing marks a lazy writer quicker than moldy buzzwords and mildewed phrases. Don't, for Pete's sake, even if you're in a pinch or a bind, reinvent the wheel, or fix something that ain't broke.

On Sexism in Print

As an organizational writer/editor, you're going to have to resolve a damned-if-you-do/damned-if-you-don't occupational dilemma: How not to presume maleness or femaleness in sentence constructions without seeming (1) clumsy or distracting. (2) ungrammatical, or (3) sexist.

For expressive writers, transgressions of grammar and style are far more grating than accusations of chauvinism in copy. For them, it has nothing to do with sexism and everything to do with energetic writing.

It's proper nowadays to shun words with grafted feminine endings such as authoress, sculptress, poetess, usherette, aviatrix, comedienne, and to refer instead to male and female members of groups collectively with designations that used to imply the male gender: author, sculptor, poet, usher, aviator, comedian. There are the inevitable exceptions: "actress," "waitress," "divorcée" to name just a few in a burgeoning list, and editors must be alert to them.

Now standard as well is the substitution of neutral words or phrases such as "reporter," "leader," "sales representative" — for titles and descriptions that assume maleness when both sexes are represented: "newsman," "chairman," "salesman."

"Homemakers" have displaced "housewives." And it's passé to employ terms of comeliness when they're not essential to the thought being conveyed. Unintentionally or not, calling attention to a woman's physical attributes — or lack of them — reduces her, in the mind of many, to a sex object or, perhaps worse, a sexless object. In kindred consideration, shun descriptive words for males such as "hunk" and "beefcake."

Remember, too, when motherhood was sainted and uncontroversial? Decades ago, *The New York Times* began advising its writers not to refer to women before the birth of their babies as "mothers," but to call them, indisputably, "pregnant women."

Verboten, too, are terms that might cast racial or religious aspersions. "Dutch treat," for example, may imply that Dutch people are cheap. "Siesta" might denote laziness to sensitive Latinos.

Even "burly," an adjective once implying ignorance, may still be offensive to some, particularly if they're burly themselves. And it's smart to avoid all mention of skin tone: "paleface," "redskin," "lily white," "blackhearted," to mention just a few.

Furthermore, in these youth-oriented times you'd be wise to forgo references to chronological age unless they're critical to your story. "Senior citizen," "silver fox," "old-timer," "blue-haired," "coot," "geezer," "matron," "curmudgeon," even "grandparent" are unwelcome reminders in our Peter Pan society of our galloping mortality. "Old" has become a modern pejorative.

Getting back to sexism in print, it gets just as sticky when words can't be substituted without drawing attention to themselves or rendering the sentence awkward. "Mankind" and "humanity" should be above reproach, but what about such longstanding words as "manhole," "management," "manhood," "manhunt," "manhandle," "manicurist," and a slew of others? Making them "neutral" by substituting "person" for "man" would make them something else. Laughable.

Another dilemma for writers involves following an indefinite antecedent that may be male or female with the pronoun "his": " good sales representative ends *his* pitch by asking for business." "A smart teacher doesn't turn his back on students." An obvious solution is to pluralize the antecedent, thus rendering the pronoun sexless: "Good sales representatives end their pitch..." "Smart teachers don't turn their backs..." At times, however, this option will dilute your copy or even alter its intended meaning.

Worse — and this has become such an increasingly common, lazy error it's become acceptable usage — writers now deliberately tack plural pronouns onto singular antecedents, as did this Eastern Airlines spokesperson in a commercial on national TV: "We're going to give the business flyer what they are demanding."

"I will state for the record that I am a firm believer that someday 'they' will be the acceptable choice for this situation," states on-line grammarian Mignon Fogarty in her excellent style guide, Gram*mar Girl's Quick and Dirty Tips for Better Writing*. "English currently lacks a word that fits the bill, and many people are already either mistakenly or purposefully using *they* as a singular gender-neutral pronoun, so it seems logical that rules will eventually move in that direction."

Nevertheless, Fogarty cautions, if you're responsible to superiors "there's a good chance at least one of them will think you are careless or ignorant if you use *they* with a singular antecedent," even though you've avoided sounding sexist."

What to do? "Rewrite your sentences to avoid the problem," counsels Fogarty. "If that's not possible, check if the people you are writing for have a style guide. If not, use *he or she* if you want to play it safe, or use *they* if you feel bold and prepared to defend yourself."

Again, the quality of all writing rests strictly in the opinion of the beholder. For a freelance writer or organizational employee, it is the judgment and approval of the individual with the final say on what gets into print and what doesn't. So live with it.

Believe in Yourself

In an episode of the TV show, *M*A''S*H*, Hawkeye Pierce is asked by a television reporter if he'd brought any books with him to Korea. "Just one," Hawkeye replies. "The dictionary. It has all the other books in it."

And a writer is a writer is a writer. During your communications career, you'll be asked to pen many things, and your answer should always be the same: "Sure, no problem, I can do it. Hey, I'm a writer."

That's your job — stringing words together, toward whatever end is asked of you, and you can do it, handle the job every time if you just believe you can, with occasional help from your friends. And the libraries, bookstores, and the Internet are full of them.

In the early days of my freelance writing career, when I couldn't afford to turn down any work regardless how busy I was, a client asked me if to come up with an inscription for a hospital cornerstone. And he had to have it by evening. No problem, I assured him, then hunkered down with my old buddy John Bartlett. I remember thumbing through his *Familiar Quotations,* copying down a line here, a line there.

I liked something I came across in a speech by Franklin D. Roosevelt: "The test of our progress is not whether we add more to the abundance of those who have much; it is whether we provide enough for those who have too little."

Then a stanza from a poem by Anderson M. Scruggs caught my eye: "Yet after brick and steel/And stone are gone/And flesh and blood are dust/The dream lives on."

And so on.

The next morning, I turned in a selection of cornerstone inscriptions to my client that were neither FDR's nor Anderson Scrugg's nor mine:

There is no progress save that forged in the spirit of human caring.

Count our progress in these bricks and mortar forged in the kiln of human compassion.

These bricks, forged in the kiln of human caring, mark our progress.

All real progress is based on a universal desire to vanquish mortal pain and suffering.

The touchstone of our progress is not whether we have added more to the abundance of those who have much, but whether we have canceled human pain and suffering regardless of need and resource.

Beyond the steel and stone and mortar, the dream lives on.

I don't know if any of this collective eloquence was ever carved into the granite of a new medical center in Beaverton, Oregon.
But I like to think so.
The important thing is I came through for a client on a writing assignment tossed at me out of left held.
And it didn't occur to me for a moment that I wouldn't succeed.

On Ebook Publishing and a Dying Industry

For all you aspiring authors out there, here's a blog worth passing on from an Internet discussion on the merits of ebooks vs. the traditional dead-tree kind, as green authors refer to them:

> I don't want to get started on why the traditional publishing industry is a dinosaur trying desperately to survive by eating its young — authors who after years of writing their books followed by years spent preparing and revising book proposals, recruiting an agent, attempting to interest a publisher, then editing and re-editing their books in lock-step compliance with the formulaic dictates of publishing house editors only to finally earn royalties based on "net" (there are no other kind anymore) that yield them literally pennies per copy.

> I said I didn't want to get started, but I will, because an estimated 95 percent of published authors don't earn a dime beyond their generic advance of a few thousand dollars. And most of that luckless majority never receive a royalty, and if they do, wind up taking many

years to pay it back. Nowadays, too, since the advent of POD publishing, traditional houses don't ever have to designate a title "out of print," thus never re-gift the publishing rights to their authors, leaving the titles to languish in forgotten dog-in-manger limbos.

So if you're writing a book, dear author, whether you aspire to sell a hundred or a million copies, if the thought of finding a traditional publishing house to do it for you even enters your mind, genuflect, cross yourself, and ask someone to slap you repeatedly until the thought flees your consciousness forever. Then put your time, energy, emotion, aspirations, and creativity back into your writing. When you're done, thanks to this glorious computer age, for a few dollars or a few dollars more if you'd prefer to hire a techie to help you through the digital hoops, your book — *your* book as per *your* vision born of *your* unique talents — *will* be published.

And you *will* earn more money, however small or munificent the amount based on the merits of your books, than you would with a traditional publisher. Most importantly, you will have spared yourself in the interim, years upon wasted years of fruitless effort, depleted creativity, esteem-diminishing rejection, and saddest of all, *time* — oh, so much precious time, energy, and emotion that could have been invested in your writing instead of squandered on a frustratingly aloof, callously self-serving industry.

So let's hear it for ebooks!

Another electronic author put a slam-dunk ending to the on-line conversation with a couple of hypothetical questions: "In this wondrous age of digital publishing and instant-delivery cyberspace bookstores, why would anyone — authors or readers — go anywhere else for their books. It's an exciting time to be a writer, wouldn't you say?"

Yes, Dorothy, because this isn't Kansas anymore. It isn't even Oz. It's the incredible world of Internet publishing, a truly magical kingdom.

Earn Your Own Respect

"Familiarity," wrote Aesop, "breeds contempt." "And children," Mark Twain added two centuries later.

True on both counts, particularly the former in today's workplace. It has struck me that only exceptional supervisors tend not to devalue, over time, the worth of those who labor in their organizational vineyards. It's called taking people for granted — a predictable human failing. Why do we all eventually come to accept excellence and exceptional effort as standards of performance, then become disgruntled when subsequent achievement dips below those standards?

In every employer-employee relationship there seems to be a honeymoon period of gratitude and appreciation followed by a gradual deterioration of esteem. Maybe it has to do with appreciation obligating reward. And by devaluing worth, we lessen obligation, which is why the American Dream really isn't about fame and fortune. it's about being your own boss, a state of grace only a few of us are privileged to attain.

The point is, you must keep faith in yourself. If you don't, no one else will. Let your confidence in your skills, your talent, and your worth be shaken by one person only — the writer who walks around in your skin.